Be Different:

Finding the Resilience to Lead

Published by Christopher Howard and Andrew Gross

And we rejoice in the hope of the glory of God. Not only so, but we also rejoice in our sufferings, because we know that suffering produces perseverance; perseverance, character; and character, hope. And hope does not disappoint us, because God has poured out His love into our hearts by the Holy Spirit whom He has given us.
Romans 5:2-5

Chris — This book is dedicated to my best friend and loving wife Meaghan. I'm so blessed to have a partner who pushes me further in my walk with Christ and challenges me in ways that make a better husband, father and human being.

Andrew — This book is dedicated to my beautiful wife Sarah. Our marriage in Christ has been the "school of love" that has taught me all about differentiation. Thank you for being my example and tutor.

Table of Contents

Part I: What is the Biblically Differentiated Self?

Chapter One: Say What? 1

Chapter Two: Embrace the Created Self 32

Chapter Three: Embrace the Re-created Self.............. 63

Chapter Four: Embrace the Self-in-Relation 96

Chapter Five: Jesus, the Differentiated and
Differentiating One 124

Part II: Some Practical Advice

Chapter Six: Make Use Most of the Hard Stuff 162

Chapter Seven: Nurture Your Created Self 216

Chapter Eight: Nurture Your Re-created Self............... 256

Chapter Nine: Nurture Your Self-in-Relation................ 271

Chapter Ten: Alfonso, Petr and Jennifer 328

Epilogue 335

Part I:

What is the Biblically Differentiated Self?

Chapter One:
Say What?

Alfonso, Petr, and Jennifer

"I think Petr's serious this time, Al ... about killing himself ... and I, I just have no idea where he is..." Jennifer's voice was trembling, but she managed to choke out, "Please, Al... I just don't know what to do..."

"OK, OK. Just calm down, Jen," Alfonso vainly tried to keep his own voice calm. "Can you just first tell me what happened?"

Through intermittent sobs, Jennifer began to tell Alfonso how her husband, Petr Wolansky, had disappeared. When she'd woken that morning he was gone. He hadn't taken the car, his wallet or phone. Only some cash was gone. He'd left a note that threatened suicide two days from now, on his 45th birthday. The note gave no hint of his whereabouts.

Alfonso Sanchez, Petr's best friend since their days together as missionaries in Tanzania, East Africa, held the phone with one hand and

1

his head with his other. The room felt like it was swimming around him. He was stunned at this turn of events. How could Petr, the most gifted, anointed and dynamic preacher and church leader he knew, have gone off the deep end like this? Like Petr, Alfonso was also a busy pastor of a medium sized church, and was facing his own host of personal and ministry challenges at the moment. But all that seemed to stand still at the thought that his best friend was wandering around somewhere and seriously ready to end his own life.

"Alfonso, I haven't told anyone else about this. No one else has any idea that there is a problem. They all think we are so happy and that everything at the church is going so successfully. Honestly, Alfonso, I think you're the only person he ever confided in. You're like the only person he was really honest with about his problems. You've got to help Alfonso! I just don't know where else to turn."

"Jen, please, calm down. I'm going to help, but I'm trying to think. Please, just give me a moment to think." Alfonso normally couldn't think this quickly, and wanted some extra time to get his mind around what was happening.

If he left now and drove the two hours to Indianapolis to help out, he'd miss his son's big championship soccer game.

But there might be worse trouble if he had to find someone else to do that wedding for him on Friday. The board would not be happy about that at all, since the bride-to-be was a board member's daughter. What should he do? Helping find Petr would disrupt everything. But isn't this what real friends do for each other? Wasn't that the right thing to do?

"Jen, I'll come down. I can be there by mid-morning." If he left now, would he even have time to grab coffee at his favorite coffee shop? If there was ever a day Alfonso needed his coffee, it was today.

"Oh, Alfonso, really? Oh, thank you so much. I truly don't have anyone else to turn to…"

"But Jen," Alfonso interrupted, "I'm going to ask you to be really, really brave right now, and to do some really hard things while you're waiting for me to get there."

"Anything, Alfonso."

"Jen, you need to look through his files — look on his computer and go through his emails. You'll need to go through all his recent Facebook postings. And you said he left his phone there?"

"That's right."

"OK, so we'll need to go through his texts too. We've got to start combing through everything and see if he's left any clues about where he could be right now. So Jen, while you're waiting for me, I need you to start doing this.

"I realize that this is going to be really hard to do, but it might be our only chance to figure out where he could be, and we can't waste any time. We've got to use every minute… Do you understand?"

There was a long pause on the other end of the phone. Jennifer swallowed, took a deep breath, and then said with a stammering voice: "Yep. I'll do whatever it takes Alfonso."

"Do the kids know what's going on Jen?" Alfonso asked after another long pause.

"No, Alfonso. They don't." She started crying again, softly this time. "I haven't told the kids anything. Just now, right before I called you, I got them ready for school and sent them off to the bus stop as if nothing was different. I held it together that whole time, but the second they were gone I called you immediately, and that's when I just lost it Al. I don't know if I should tell them or not. You have no idea what this'll do to them. Oh, Alfonso, I just can't think straight right now. They've known for a while now that their dad's been having a really hard time. But I think this would crush them. And little Sofia … Oh! Alfonso, I mean, if little Sofia were to lose her daddy…" Jennifer broke down and sobbed.

"OK, OK, so Jen, let's not tell them just yet. Of course you're having a hard time thinking straight. Who wouldn't be in these circumstances?"

He drew a deep breath, "You'll wait at home till I get there, right? Let's pray and maybe God will show us some direction to take with the kids. Just take a deep breath right now, OK?"

"Oh Alfonso…."

"I know, I know. I am so, so sorry that this is happening Jen. Hey, let's pray, OK? Have you prayed at all yet?"

"I, I haven't. I just haven't even known how…I just don't know where to begin…I mean, if God could let this happen, then how can we… how can we…"

"I know, I know Jen. Let me pray right now, OK?

The two quietly bowed their heads as Alfonso let out an impassioned plea for God to spare Petr's life. It was one of those prayers from the gut. Alfonso, used to filtering out anger or fear or doubt for public consumption when he prayed, was surprised at the desperate sound in his voice. When they were finished, neither felt much better. But Alfonso had the tiniest glimmer of hope. Maybe, just maybe, they could get to Petr in time.

Why Was Petr In Trouble?

Why was Petr in trouble? What was he missing that made his trials so hard for him? Why did his life crumble into despair and attempted suicide when the pressures of life and ministry became too much?

Petr's challenges were many and hard, as you'll soon discover. But they were also normal challenges, in the sense that most people face trials of the same severity at one time or another. Those who lead Christian ministries especially can count on facing challenges, even extreme ones, because more than most they get swept up into other peoples' trials.

One would think that Petr was equipped to face these hardships, since, as his friend Alfonso testified, he was "the most gifted, anointed and dynamic preacher and church leader he knew." How could someone with such talent and ability succumb to life's extreme, but normal, pressures?

Why do some Christian leaders handle life's pressures with resilience, but others fail miserably under the same pressures? Some come back stronger than ever, thriving and transformed into better people. But others inwardly collapse or implode. Some discover hope for the long haul and the resilience to lead, but others don't. Why? What was Petr missing? What are other people missing who implode?

We believe that a core element of surviving trials with resilience is to cultivate a *biblical differentiation of self.*

Say what?

You may not be familiar with the word "differentiation." It has mainly been used by professional psychotherapists and psychologists in specialized therapy settings.

You won't find the word itself in Scripture if you try to look it up with the best concordance in the world. But we think it is a very biblical concept.

Differentiation is a term coined about sixty years ago by therapist Murray Bowen. He used it to describe a person's emotional maturity. By this he meant the ability to manage your emotions, your thoughts, your relationships and your very identity in ways that positively impact other people. He talked about how differentiation can help you be what he called a "non-anxious presence," or a calm, peaceful person, in the midst of stress, pain and rancor.

In Christian terms, this means having no inner hindrances to loving people the way God commands you to love them. It means that you're able to manage your inner life in such a way that you can obey Jesus' command to lay down your life in love for others, just like He did (John 15:12, Eph. 5:1). This mainly involves being faithful, in the power of the Holy Spirit, to being the real you, the "you" created and recreated by God Himself, for His glory. If you're faithful to being the real you, then you can be free from the control of people and circumstances and inner obstacles that threaten to knock you off the path of obedience and effective leadership.

As these chapters unfold, you'll get a better picture of what all this means for you practically. In the meantime, consider the following ways in which differentiation might help you become a more resilient and persevering person.

Frequently, when a trial hits us, we don't just suffer from the trial itself. Our suffering is magnified beyond the actual trial because it threatens to take something deeply precious from us — something from our sense of identity.

For example, if a ship sinks in the ocean, its surviving captain suffers not only from the loss of the ship, the loss of cargo and possibly the loss of passengers and crew; he suffers even more deeply from the fact that the accident now potentially labels him a failure as a ship's captain. His competence is called into question, leaving him open to the accusation that his significance and worth as a person have failed. He suffers doubly, once from the actual accident, and twice from how the incident robs something essential from his identity.

This double suffering is particularly acute if the trial involves relationships. For instance, think of how deeply you can suffer if a hardship earns you the disapproval of your spouse. Maybe you've hit a financial difficulty, and it launches your spouse into a bitter tirade over your perceived mismanagement of funds. Sound familiar?

In this situation, you not only suffer because of the situation itself — you suffer from the fact that now you're the bad guy.

You feel no better than a criminal in the other's eyes. The suffering compounds because your precious and deeply held sense of self, your belief that you're basically a good and faithful spouse, is at risk from your spouse's disapproval. He or she has vilified you, and not only must you recover from the pain of the financial situation—now you must recover from the pain of your newly criminalized identity.

And how do you recover from a wound to your identity? How do you recover if the other person wields your identity's most feared weapon: disapproval? And for the Christian who endeavors to follow Jesus, how do you recover so that you can again offer your spouse the love He commands of you?

But if you're a highly differentiated person, you cannot be controlled by other people and their approval or disapproval, even if you are partially to blame for some of your problems. This is because a highly differentiated person has a strong sense of self that cannot be pushed around easily by others' opinions. If you are highly differentiated, even the opinions of your spouse or your most intimate friends and relatives can't push your around easily.

And if you can't be pushed around by disapproval, you will be able to love people the way Jesus commands you to love them. A lot of times, Jesus' command to love certain people sets off an automatic, inner recoil: "I'll love anyone but *her*, Jesus!" A thousand excuses and justifications rise up inside of us about why it is OK not to love this person or that person as Jesus orders.

But a highly differentiated person can be free from this automatic recoil.

How? Simply put, a well-differentiated person sees him or herself as *different* than, and not dependent upon or at one with, the shifting sands of other peoples' favor or disfavor. That's where the word "differentiation" comes from: a person's selfhood is *different* than others' approval or disapproval.

Therefore, like a thick, healthy oak tree, a well-differentiated person's sense of self, or identity, feels solid and unmovable. A strong sense of self knows how to stay firmly rooted in truth, even when a storm of disapproval strips you of all your leaves and branches. So, when the storm of another's disapproval threatens to wash away or crush your identity, you can calmly endure it. You have the quiet confidence that the danger will eventually pass and that your selfhood will remain intact.

If there has been damage, new growth will come in time because a firmly planted tree can eventually sprout new leaves and branches. Strangely, you can even rejoice because perhaps you'll end up better off for having gone through the purging of the storm.

But people with a low level of differentiation are deeply tortured when their identities are attacked or damaged during a trial or difficulty. In the above scenario of financial troubles, people with low differentiation tend to react anywhere along a spectrum of negative behaviors. On the one end of the spectrum, some fight back with even more criminalizing vitriol: "Well, I wouldn't have misspent that money if you hadn't been so miserly!" These fighters react with defensive maneuvers to the perceived attack on their identities. It's common to react this way, since attacks to your identity can make you feel like you're on the defense for your very survival. This is when all responses feel justified, from biting sarcasm and scathing remarks to screaming, verbal abuse, and even violence.

On the other end of the spectrum, people inwardly collapse in despair: "life's over!" These collapsers react to the perceived attack by shrinking away and withering up. They feel as if the attackers have exposed evidence that they are worthless. This can be one cause of the kind of intractable depression we encounter so frequently in people, in which a person feels hopelessly flawed and without remedy.

Most of us fall somewhere on the spectrum between the two extremes, depending on factors like upbringing, culture, circumstances and personality. On both ends of the spectrum the anxiety over gaining another's approval or the worry over losing that approval can exert enormous impact on us and shape how we react, even against our better judgment.

Needless to say, the first casualty of reacting either as a fighter or a collapser is Jesus' command to love in imitation of His love.

We're sure you've seen the devastation that can result when leaders, and especially church leaders, react at either end of this spectrum. If leaders react with anger and recriminations, they lose the trust and respect of followers. If leaders react by wilting into a passive lump, they also lose the trust and respect of followers.

But those with higher levels of differentiation are free to step away from the entire spectrum of poor reactions. They have the freedom to choose other responses.

For the Christian who wants to follow Jesus' command to love our neighbors, love even our enemies, wouldn't it be wonderful to have the freedom to respond with love? What if we could respond this way, even when feeling threatened by another's disapproval, instead of responding with either rage or despair?

Wouldn't it be wonderful to feel so comfortable and confident with your real self that it doesn't endanger you when someone dislikes you, impugns your character, calls your integrity into question, casts doubt on your suitability for a job, or in some way challenges your deeply held beliefs about yourself?

Differentiation is the key to responding with this freedom instead of reacting from somewhere on the spectrum of negative behaviors.

But instead of cultivating higher levels of differentiation, what most of us do is fortify and project a false sense of self. In the face of threats to our identity, we construct a more or less fabricated image for public consumption. We feel that if others see an image of us that is more winsome than the ugly reality, we won't be so victimized by their disapproval. We spend an enormous amount of time and energy strengthening and broadcasting this false self, however disingenuous it may be. It feels as if others won't have cause to damage our precious identity if they observe something more alluring than reality.

Therefore, we pour a lot into building and managing this image, which we believe has the power to win approval and fend off disapproval.

This image is more than just putting our "best foot forward," normally a good practice depending on the circumstance. It is a public relations spin designed mainly to impress with smoke and mirrors. Unfortunately, even though parts of this image may express the real self underneath it all, much of the image is a floppy contrivance that can't withstand the average hardships of life. It is so flimsy that it can be taken down with even moderate levels of scrutiny. And trials and difficulties always serve to scrutinize what we're really made of.

But most of us are unaware that there's a difference between our real selves and our projected selves. A large part of the human tragedy is that, from an early age in childhood, we confuse our real identities with this false, projected image. We assume that the projected self is in fact the real self. This confusion leads to endless trouble over a lifetime. Though it is designed to defend the real self, the projected self ends up endangering our identities because we divert resources from nourishing the real self and instead pour them into the projected self.

The strength for surviving and thriving through trials comes from staying rooted in and faithful to the real self that God created and then re-created in Christ. Therefore, every time we starve the real self to feed the false, projected self, we weaken our own ability to be resilient in trials.

People who cultivate their real selves strengthen their capacity to endure trials in a successful way. They even can learn the art of benefiting from trials, as we will discuss later in Chapter 6. Improving your level of differentiation is a big part of gaining this capacity. Having higher levels of differentiation means that you can be more true to God and to the person God has called you to be. It means that you can be more true to the life mission that God has given you.

You can begin to see from the examples above how a person with higher differentiation can bounce back more fully and quickly when hardships come his or her way. It enables you to be calm and peaceful in stressful situations and with stressful relationships, because they no longer pose a threat to your deepest sense of identity. Ultimately, being differentiated frees you up to love people as Jesus commanded, even those whom you might otherwise find difficult to love.

But if you have a low level of differentiation, you get stressed more easily, by situations and by people. You tend to lose perspective during stressful times and you more easily react with negative emotions. This makes you more easily controlled by others; both by those you dislike and by those you love. Ultimately it makes it hard for you to love people as Jesus commanded.

Those you dislike can feel personally threatening if you have a low level of differentiation. This is because it can feel as if they could rob you of something deeply precious, something from your very identity. A bully's insults aren't mere words. They can cut us to the heart because it feels as if they can violate our defenses and steal something integral to our very self.

Surprisingly, those you love can also arouse anxiety and make you feel personally threatened if your level of differentiation is low. How? It is because we often feel anxious about gaining and keeping the approval of those we love.

The love others seems like a treasure too good to lose. It demands our vigilance to protect it. This anxious vigilance acts like a chain, determining our attitudes, reactions and behavior.

So staying true to yourself, to being the person God has made you to be, and staying true to God's agenda in your life, can feel more challenging to a less differentiated person. It is harder to manage your emotions constructively if you are consumed with gaining human approval or warding off threatening people.

All this control by others makes a person far more vulnerable to the kind of implosion that Petr is going through, as we'll soon see. Worse yet for the Christian who wants to follow Jesus, it makes it elusive to love people the way He commands.

How is Any of This Christian?

Discerning Christians will ask at this point, "Why do we need to introduce yet another fancy term from professional psychology to help Christian leaders? Doesn't Scripture alone contain enough wisdom for our sanctification, our emotional maturity, and our leadership competence?"

Christianity has always cherished a very similar idea to Bowen's "differentiation." But instead of using that word, throughout the history of the church we've described highly differentiated people by saying things like, "That woman is not afraid to tell people the hard truth, because she only fears the Lord and not human opinion;" or, "That fellow stood up for what was right, even though it cost him everything he had;" or, "She can love even the most unlovable person;" or, "I'm amazed at how that man chooses to respond to injustice with love instead of revenge," or "how can she remain so calm and peaceful when her life is crashing down around her?"

David is one example of a person who demonstrated a high level of differentiation for many parts of his life. He showed this differentiation from an early age; starting the day he brought provisions to his brothers from the family farm (1 Sam. 17:17-20). His oldest brother Eliab accused him of foolishly neglecting his duties and chasing after the thrill of seeing a battle. He said to David: "I know your insolence and the wickedness of your heart" (1 Sam. 17:38). A less differentiated person might feel crushed by the accusation and the disapproval of an older, admired brother. At this point, Eliab's opinion of David might have easily shaped his next set of actions in a negative way. What if David had left the army camp at that moment because he felt ashamed by his brother's untrue but stinging rebuke? But David confidently pushed aside anxiety over Eliab's disapproval and pursued doing what was right.

David again showed differentiation later that same day when he confronted Goliath. If David had been a less differentiated person, he might have quickly succumbed to the attitude of the whole Israelite army. He might have ridden their roller coaster of fear all the way to their paralysis of action. Instead, David was differentiated from the Israelite army, so he resolutely and calmly decided to do what was right, trusting God to be with him in the face of great risk (1 Sam. 17:31-58).

The prophet Nathan showed a high level of differentiation from David's approval when he confronted the king for his sin with Bathsheba and Uriah (2 Sam. 11-12:1-15). What sane person confronts a king who holds the power to arbitrarily execute his opponents? But instead of worrying about the king's approval or disapproval, Nathan confidently delivered his blistering message from God.

In sharp contrast, King Saul demonstrated again and again his very low level of differentiation. Saul's confidence as leader of the Israelites was bound up inseparably with the approval of his people. Think of how he wrongly jumped to assume Samuel's priestly duties when Samuel was late, out of fear of losing the crowd's attention and approval (1 Sam 13:5-14). He was motivated mainly to win their admiration in that moment. Or think of Saul's unwillingness to stop his people from seizing the spoils of their victory over the Amalekites, against the express order of God (compare 1 Sam. 15:3 to 1 Sam. 15:20-21). He was motivated to do whatever would most likely get the people's endorsement in that instance, in spite of the Lord's command. Think of Saul's burning jealousy and resulting paranoia when he felt he was losing the public's favor to David's rising star (1 Sam. 18:5-9). In each case, Saul had intertwined his sense of self too closely with the high esteem or low esteem of his people. Their support, not God's, determined his behavior and actions.

Centuries later, the prophet Habakkuk exhibited strong differentiation when God gave him a vision of a coming disaster. Habakkuk foresaw a time when Israel, deservedly, would suffer from an invasion by proud heathens. Worse yet, extreme agricultural failure was prophesied to accompany this coming catastrophe: "the fig tree does not bud, there are no grapes on the vine, the olive crop fails, the fields produce no food," and "there are no sheep in the pen and no cattle in the stalls" (Hab. 3:16-17). He admits that when he heard of this coming event, his "heart pounded," his "lips quivered," "decay crept into my bones" and his "legs trembled." But Habakkuk could also testify to waiting "*patiently* for the day of calamity" (vs. 16). He then stated firmly, "yet I will rejoice in the Lord, I will be joyful in God my Savior" (vs. 18).

The prophet then uses an unusual image to describe this ability to rejoice in the face of great disaster; in verse 19 he says that God "makes my feet like the feet of the deer, he enables me to tread on the heights." This reference evokes the image of the red deer of the Middle East making impossible progress up a sheer, nearly vertical cliff face. God was promising Habakkuk that He would enable him to scale the impossible cliff of suffering with joyful freedom.

Against all reason, God would empower him to be differentiated from his own suffering and from the suffering of his own people so that he would not get swallowed up by despair when the terrible day came.

The New Testament is full of other instances of well-differentiated people. Think of Stephen, the first Christian martyr. In Acts 7:2-53, Stephen boldly declares the Gospel, which includes a stinging rebuke of his audience's misapplication of the lessons of Jewish history. When they began to stone him in their rage, Stephen miraculously interceded on their behalf with God, "Lord, do not hold this sin against them" (7:60). Differentiation was evident in his ability to be bold when facing those who threatened him. It was also evident in his ability to intercede for his enemies.

In high-pressure situations like the one Stephen faced, well-differentiated people can inwardly extract themselves from turmoil and behave according to their values no matter what the cost. Stephen could be uncompromisingly bold and he could demonstrate compassion toward the very enemies who were taking his life.

Are you beginning to see why we think differentiation can help you be a more resilient leader, especially a Christian leader?

We're sure you can quickly think of at least a dozen other examples from Scripture of people who were enabled to do mighty things for God because they were not afraid of the people who opposed them and the dangers that threatened them. And there is no shortage of biblical scoundrels whose wickedness stemmed from a low level of differentiation.

Beyond human examples in Scripture, we believe this idea is woven into God's very nature. The supreme mystery of the Christian faith, God's Trinitarian nature, actually gives us glimpses of differentiation. The Trinity is too big a topic to take on for a book this little. But for now, consider this: The perfect unity within the Trinity is possible because of the *distinctions* between its Members. In other words, the differentiation between each Member causes their unity.

For example, the Trinity was unified in Their purpose at creation, but God decided to divvy up the tasks involved: the Father spoke everything into existence (Gen. 1:3-26); the Son, as the Father's Word, carried out this command to create (John 1:3); and the Spirit, as God's breath, filled (and continues to fill) the creation with life (Gen. 1:2, Ps. 104:30).

This differentiation in tasks happens again with our salvation: the Father initiates our salvation (Eph. 1:4-5) and sends His Son to do the job (John 3:16); the Son Himself saves us by laying down His life (1 Tim. 1:15); the Spirit seals us (Eph. 1:13) and regenerates and renews us (Tit. 3:5). Somehow, mysteriously, the Trinity's unity in purpose stems from the differences of the Members.

Take some time to study Jesus' prayer in John 17. Notice how many times the unity between the Father and Son is mentioned. But notice also how they achieve this unity. Because they are different from One Another, they are able to exchange glory with One Another ("Father ... Glorify you Son, that your Son may glorify you" – vs. 1, see also vv. 4-5). Notice all the other things they exchange with One Another in this prayer. The exchange can happen because they are different. By executing different functions, the Trinitarian Members are able to support and bolster One Another the their common purpose. Their unity flows from their differentiation.

Likewise, in imitation of the Trinity, human unity in relationships stems from the ability to be differentiated from one another, as we will see later in the book. Paul hints at this connection when he points to the Trinity as the model for differentiation in marriage relationships in 1 Corinthians 11:3 and Ephesians 5:23-24.

We see this in Adam and Eve's relationship. God made Eve by removing Adam's rib (Gen. 2:21-22). He creates a "suitable helper" by *differentiating* a part of Adam from himself. Then, only after Eve has become a fully formed human can they again become "united" and "become one flesh" (vs. 24). Humanity goes from undistinguished whole, to differentiated beings, to unity again. Why this middle step of differentiation if they end up "one flesh" in the end?

This passage ends by making it clear that this is a pattern for all marriages. Differentiation is a part of God's original design to achieve intimacy in marriage, as well as in all human relationships.

Above all, Jesus was the perfect example of differentiation throughout His earthly ministry. Even when young, He brushed off his parents' rebuke for staying behind at the Temple (Luke 2:41-52). Later, His family's disapproval didn't stop him from doing the right thing, even though they were sure at one point that He was crazy (Mark 3:21).

In fact, Jesus never once held back from saying or doing the right thing, even as pressure to stop or shut up grew beyond his family to include the publically revered religious leaders. Even His endurance of the cross was an example of differentiation, as we'll explain later.

The examples are so numerous that to rehearse them would be nearly to re-write all four Gospels. We will share a selection of examples of Jesus' differentiation later in Chapter Five.

So, even though the church has rarely called it "differentiation," the insights from Bowen and other psychologists are helpful. They describe what Scripture has always identified as a key quality in the people it upholds as exemplars. It is too simplistic to call it "courage," because we're talking about that indefinable quality that is underneath courage. It is inadequate to call it "perseverance," because we're talking about the fertile soil that lets perseverance grow and flourish. It isn't simple faith or trust in God, because it is that thing that sets us free to believe.

We think the best term is "differentiation." So, we've borrowed it, along with some other terms and ideas from mainstream psychology, to help us unpack what we believe has always been a very biblical idea.

Why We're Interested

One of us (Chris) is a university professor who teaches and conducts research for a living. One of us (Andrew) is a pastor.

I (Chris) teach future business leaders and conduct seminars and workshops in Europe on global strategic thinking and building cross-cultural teams. The other one of us (Andrew) is a pastor at a multi-ethnic church where everything depends on leaders persevering through tricky relationships.

We both have poured our lives into making Christian leaders successful. Thus, we both have a vested interest in understanding why some Christian leaders crash and burn when going through trials, but why others emerge from trials better than before. Our whole lives are dedicated to producing this second kind of Christian leader.

We know the Bible has a lot to say about this topic, but I (Chris) wanted to see if modern-day research could confirm what we already know to be true from Scripture. I wanted to investigate this idea that I already saw in the Bible—that differentiation makes a person courageous, persevering and resilient in the face of hardship and ultimately more capable of loving like God wants us to love.

So a few years ago, I (Chris) conducted a research study with present-day leaders and discovered that they tend to thrive and show resilience during trials *if* they have a high level of differentiation.

But those with a lower level of different-iation generally fail to thrive when suffering. This book is actually based on this original research of mine into leadership resiliency.[1]

I was so inspired by these findings that I wanted to turn my research into a book that anybody could read. I think the findings are so important that everybody should have access to them.

Then I met Andrew, who was eager to encourage the resiliency of his fellow pastors. He is also a writer who specializes in turning academic writing into popularly accessible writing. And so a great partnership was born.

We think you're going to benefit enormously from better understanding and practicing biblical differentiation. We believe it will help you be more resilient. But it will also help you be a more effective leader because it will increase your ability to manage and motivate yourself.

---

[1] "The Impact of Obstacles and Developmental Experiences in Resilience in Leadership Formation," *American Society of Business and Behavioral Sciences*, 20, no. 1 (2013), 679-687
http://asbbs.org/files/ASBBS2013V1/PDF/H/Howard_Irving(679-687).pdf

People are drawn to and put more trust in leaders who they sense can control their own emotions and can keep themselves motivated, especially when under fire. Think back to the leaders in your life whom you've most respected. You can be one of those leaders.

If you lead a church, the stakes for leading well and leading the right way are that much higher. Don't you owe it to God, to the church, and to yourself to improve your leadership?

And even if you don't consider yourself a leader, this book is still important to you. Resilience is just another word for "perseverance," and every believer must learn how to persevere. It doesn't take much investigation into the Bible to realize that God wants to train you to persevere.

Jesus told His disciples "the one who stands firm to the end will be saved" (Matt. 24:13). Paul told the Corinthians that perseverance was one of the traits of love (1 Cor. 13:7). He wrote to Timothy that he ought to "persevere" in rightly living his life and teaching God's word "because if you do, you will save both yourself and your hearers" (1 Tim. 4:16). He told the Thessalonians that he boasted about their perseverance to other churches (2 Thess. 1:4).

Peter listed "perseverance" as one of the key characteristics necessary to keep from being "ineffective and unproductive in your knowledge of the Lord Jesus Christ" (2 Pet. 1:6). The author of Hebrews wrote: "You need to persevere so that when you have done the will of God, you will receive what He has promised" (Heb. 10:36). James showed his readers how perseverance was necessary "so that you may be mature and complete, not lacking anything" (James 1:4).

We could go on and on. But let's take a closer look at just one passage in particular. In Paul's letter to the Romans, he explained to the Romans that perseverance was part of God's way of building His people's character and hope (Rom. 5:4). He writes:

> *We rejoice in our sufferings because we know that suffering produces perseverance; perseverance, character; and character, hope. And hope does not disappoint us, because God has poured out His love into our hearts by the Holy Spirit.*

To arrive at this resilient hope, the kind of hope that doesn't disappoint, in which we experience the love of God in our hearts, Paul says that we must go through a process that includes suffering.

Somehow this suffering trains us to persevere, and that perseverance shapes our character in such a way that we can experience the non-disappointing hope.

This book is about how those sufferings produce perseverance so you can walk in that kind of hope.

We could have written an entire book just on perseverance. But you get the point. Perseverance is a necessary part of the Christian life, and you need to learn how to do it. Andrew, the pastor, thinks every day of how to motivate his congregants to persevere. He envisions a coming time when Christians will need to know how to persevere more than ever because of the pressures they will face in our world. Chris is likewise deeply concerned that the future leaders in whom he invests will one day have what it takes to last into the future.

Biblical differentiation is a critical part of learning to persevere.

How This Book Works

In Part One of the book, we're going to introduce you to the three elements of biblical differentiation.

The first element is to embrace the *created self*, or embrace the full *you* that God created, with all your unique qualities, both the positive ones you don't mind showing to the world, and even the negative ones you'd rather the world didn't see.

The second element is to embrace the *re-created self*, or the new you that God has re-created in Christ. You've probably learned and even taught others about the believer's new identity in Christ. But you probably don't need us to tell you that even the most mature followers of Jesus struggle to apply parts of that new identity.

The third element of biblical differentiation is to embrace the *self-in-relation* to the Creator and to the created. In simplest terms, this means learning to walk relationally with God and with others.

Each of these elements forms an essential leg of a three-legged stool:

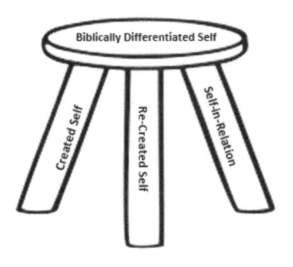

Each leg in this stool is necessary for biblical differentiation.

Part One ends with a chapter on how Jesus modeled biblical differentiation and how He made Himself the means of attaining it. This is critical because Jesus tells us He is "the way," (John 14:6) and that He expects us to follow and imitate Him (Matt. 10:38, John 10:27, 12:27). What could be more practical for professing disciples of Jesus than to look at Jesus' example and to receive His power to be transformed?

The second half of the book explains what you can do practically to cultivate a more biblically differentiated self. It starts with Chapter Six, which comes directly from Chris's original research. It explains in plain language how you can use hard life assignments, hard relationships, hard experiences, and hard training opportunities to increase your level of differentiation. Chapters Seven through Ten further explore ways to nurture the three legs of a biblically differentiated self.

Each chapter starts with the unfolding story of Alfonso, Petr, and Jennifer. Along with Alfonso and Jennifer, you will attempt to track down clues of Petr's whereabouts in the hope of rescuing him before it is too late. Will they be successful, or will their efforts be in vain?

Chapter Two:
Embrace the Created Self

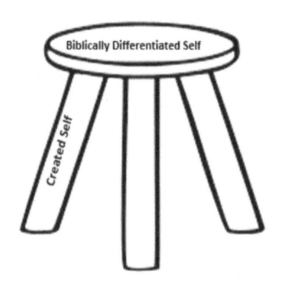

Alfonso, Petr and Jennifer

Alfonso rang the doorbell of Petr and Jennifer's front door. Jennifer buried her face in his arms.

"Al, I've been holding it together all morning, trying to keep it under control so that I can focus. Oh Al, I am so afraid…"

"It's OK, Jen. We're going to get through this," Alfonso muttered, not terribly confident about this statement. But he knew that grieving people needed others to at least sound confident.

"Oh Alfonso, going through Petr's things has just been agonizing! It makes me feel like he's so close. But at the same time it makes me feel as he's totally out of reach."

"Jen, I am so, so sorry," replied Alfonso, barely remembering to act pastorally. In most crises like this, he was able to kick into pastor-mode. It had become easy for him to do that over the years. But the imminent danger of his best friend made things different. "I understand how hard this is Jen." He paused and took a deep breath. As exhausting as the long drive had been, it had helped him delay dealing with Petr's potential suicide. After another pause he asked: "Kids are still in school?"

"Yes, and my sister's going to pick them up from school and keep them overnight, so I can put off telling them what's going on for at least a little bit."

"Good. Have you found anything yet by looking through his stuff? Actually, first I better ask if you have any coffee. I'm desperate at this point. I didn't have time to grab any after I flew out the door on my way here."

They went into the kitchen where Jennifer poured Alfonso a cup of cold coffee, reheating it in the microwave. The kitchen table was strewn with papers, letters, bills and little notes.

"I started to go through Petr's bills, to see if there was anything strange with his recent purchases." Jennifer assumed a more business-like tone and started talking a mile a minute: "I'm not sure I'm making much progress. He didn't keep many details of the places he frequented. I know he liked to go down to the coffee shop that's on the way to church. I called there first thing and asked if anyone had seen him, but he hasn't been there in days."

"OK, OK, now slow down Jen." Alfonso took his first sip of coffee and tried to breath more slowly. It tasted horrible. He'd forgotten that Jen made weak coffee. What was he going to do without decent coffee? The two hour drive here had been harrowing and exhausting, and Alfonso was no better prepared to think clearly than he had been when he'd first got the call from Jennifer. He contemplated whether he ought to get back in the car and head to that coffee shop he'd seen when getting off the freeway.

"Jen, I was more thinking that we might find some clues about what led him to this point. You know, like trying to reconstruct his recent thoughts and feelings. I figured that if we could do that, we'd get a better sense of what kind of state he's in."

"Alfonso, that is exactly what I'm most scared to find out. I mean, what if this all has to do with me? I mean, we fought a lot recently. What if somehow… What if *I* drove him to this?" A huge sob welled up and Jennifer stopped talking.

Fortunately, his pastoral instincts were now starting to kick in, and comforting Jennifer actually helped Alfonso clear his head a bit. He put his arm around her and just sat with her for a while as she cried. Finally, Alfonso calmly asked: "Let's start with the note he left, OK?"

"Oh, that!" said Jen. "I am so sick of re-reading that stupid thing — here." Jen handed him the little paper that had obviously been crumpled up, straightened, and re-crumpled at least a dozen times already.

Alfonso looked it over several times, but there were no obvious details that could reveal Petr's whereabouts. But one phrase did catch his attention: "I'm trapped in an unending nightmare." These words were exactly the ones Petr had used several times in their most recent conversations and in several recent emails and texts. In fact, Alfonso had heard Petr use this phrase so many times lately that he'd almost thought of it as Petr's new little mantra.

Memories of these recent emails and conversations started coming back to Alfonso as he stared at the note, and suddenly a light bulb went on for him.

Almost every time Petr had said those words about being trapped in an unending nightmare, he'd also quoted what had always been one of his favorite verses, 1 Corinthians 9:22: "I have become all things to all people so that by all possible means I might save some."

This memory suddenly seemed like an important connection. Alfonso remembered how, back when they had been missionaries together in Africa, he had been so impressed when Petr used to quote this verse. Back then it seemed like a sign of strong faith. At the time, he had understood Petr to mean: "I'm willing to do whatever it takes, no matter the sacrifice, to communicate the Gospel." Alfonso had found Petr's sentiment inspiring, because it seemed so much like Jesus to be willing to sacrifice his culture and even personality to win others for God. It felt so noble and virtuous back then.

But recently, it had been bothering him. Over the last couple years, and especially lately, Petr's association between the verse and the phrase "trapped in an unending nightmare" had become common. Now a new connection clicked in his brain. One recent conversation stood out in his memory.

"Alfonso," he remembered Petr pleading: "How can I be so miserable? I'm just trying to follow God's call to be 'all things to all people?' But I keep getting more and more unhappy. Instead of feeling good about it all, I feel like I'm trapped inside an unending nightmare."

Petr had gone on: "For example, every time John, the church board chair I've told you about, gets hostile, I try to respond with the mindset of 1 Corinthians 9:22. But that only seems to make him angrier and less satisfied with my leadership. It's like he finds more faults with me the more I try to appease him by being 'all things' to him. Ahhg! It just all makes me feel so trapped Al."

Alfonso now recalled why this conversation had made him feel uncomfortable. He knew that, even though following God's direction could get a person into hot water, there was still supposed to be inner peace and joy. Where was Petr's inner and peace and joy if he were really following 1 Corinthians 9:22? Something had started to feel off about how Petr interpreted that verse, and it was somehow a clue to Petr's whereabouts.

"Jen, did Petr ever say much to you about his relationship with the board chair, John something-or-other?"

"John Remington? Oh, goodness, I think that's got to be a big source of the trouble Alfonso. They did not get along, despite all of Petr's best efforts. You know Petr; he can get along with anyone, make anyone feel happy. He's so charming. That's why the congregation has always loved him so much. That's why he's been successful in everything he's ever done. He can charm anybody!

"But" she wen on, "there was no pleasing John. It just crushed Petr that of all the people who couldn't be pleased, one of them was his boss."

"That's interesting, because I butt heads with my church's board chair all the time. She and I disagree more than we agree. But it doesn't crush me. I wonder why it crushed Petr?"

"Oh, you know what Petr's like Alfonso. He'll do whatever it takes to please somebody. I tell him all the time that he'd be willing to twist himself into a pretzel shape to make somebody happy. It has actually become a big issue in our marriage the last few years because sometimes I'm the casualty of that pretzel shape. But what makes me mad about the board chair is that Petr has tried so hard with him. He really went above and beyond with John. But instead of appreciating all the effort, John just got grumpier and less tolerant. I mean, doesn't it count for something that Petr went through all that trouble to be all things for him?"

"You mean, like Petr's favorite verse?"

"1 Corinthians 9:22? Yeah, that always has been Petr's favorite verse. The one about being 'all things to all people.' I think it's like his life verse or something. He quotes it all the time, ever since I've known him in fact. He found a way to get it into almost every sermon." She paused. "Why Al? What does that have to do with the note?"

"Well, I might be way off, but I think that verse is some kind of key to figuring this out Jen. Did you find his journal?"

"Yep, right here. I, I've been afraid to look at it."

It didn't take Alfonso long to find several recent entries in the journal that quoted 1 Corinthians 9:22. Alfonso glanced through them and found exactly what he expected.

"Here it is Jen. He's quoting that verse, at the same time he's talking about feeling trapped in an unending nightmare. He combined these two ideas several times in our recent conversations. Listen to this: *Why can't other people appreciate that I'm being all things to them? But when I try to follow Jesus by appeasing others, it makes me feel so trapped in an unending nightmare. How is this possible?*"

"'Unending nightmare?'" said Jennifer blankly. "Is that how he really felt about life with me? I knew it, Al ..." Tears started to role down her cheeks again.

"Jen, I really don't think it was you who was an unending nightmare," Alfonso replied calmly. "I think it was something else. Something about the way that he interpreted this verse."

"What do you mean?" asked Jen, hesitantly.

"What I mean is that Paul wasn't talking about twisting himself into a pretzel shape in order to appease people, to make people happy with him."

"Well, what else is it supposed to mean? And what does that have to do with wherever Petr might be hiding?"

"Just be patient with me Jen. Has Petr played golf recently? Has he been able to pursue is interest in motorcycles? How about his love for jigsaw puzzles? Any good books lately? I think thrillers were his favorite genre. What about his local friends? Does he ever get together with them? How about sleep? Has he been getting enough lately?

"He hasn't played golf in years, except to impress one of the rich people at church. He didn't touch that motorcycle for years because he had no time, and he finally had to sell it to pay off debt."

"Hm. Now I think I do remember him telling me about the motorcycle."

Jennifer continued, "I felt bad because that was one of the only things he did for pleasure, but we had to do it. And since when has he liked jigsaw puzzles? I've never seen him do one. Reading for pleasure? That stopped a long time ago. Local friends? Unless he's hiding something, I don't think he's seen one of them in ages."

She paused and swallowed, "Alfonso, I seriously think you're the only one of his real friends left. And sleep? Oh goodness, I don't think he gets any more than 5 hours a night, based on when he goes to bed and when he get ups. But what does any of this have to do with...?"

"Jen," asked Alfonso slowly, "why has he given up all those things? Why doesn't he get enough sleep? He's not 25 anymore."

"Oh, you know Alfonso; endless meetings at church; endless activities related to the ministry, endless communicating with people. It's got to be the same way with you. Aren't all pastors like that?"

"Mmm, not necessarily. But Jen, what *reason* does he give you for letting all this stuff go that he loves so much?"

Jennifer was silent for a long time, searching her memory. "I guess ... well, he quotes that verse all the time. Every time he has to give something up, or every time I tell him to come to bed, he'll say something like, 'I just need to be all things to all people.'"

"Hmmm. That's what I thought Jen. That's also what he says to me whenever I ask him about these sorts of things. But I think he's misusing that verse. You see, that verse does means that Paul was willing to go to any length to win someone to Christ. And I think Petr sincerely thinks he's doing that. But..."

46

"But what Al?"

"I also think that somewhere along the way, he confused that idea with this idea that he should twist himself into whatever pretzel shape he needs to, even to the point of erasing himself, just to make others happy."

"I don't get it Alfonso. What do you mean?"

"What I'm trying to say is that Petr was willing to give up his own preferences, his own interests, his own pursuits, the things that made him happy, even his basic need for sleep, all to please others. He did that in the name of 1 Corinthians 9:22. But I wonder if what was really happening was that he was insecure about the approval of others, so he used the verse to justify to himself that he ought to be trying to impress them."

Jennifer just silently stared at Al.

Al went on, "What I mean is that Petr was actually *suppressing* his created self, the person God made him to be, in order to gain the reward of human approval."

Jennifer was silent for an even longer time, starring blankly off into space. Finally, she spoke slowly: "I, I hate to admit this, but I guess I have questioned why Petr works so hard to get other people's approval. He kind of works harder at that than at anything else he does. It always seems to be the one thing that makes him feel better about himself, if he gets their approval, I mean ..."

"Yes...?"

"I mean, otherwise, he says he feels 'so empty.'.... I don't know, this doesn't make any sense, Alfonso. And what does this have to do with where he might be hiding right now?"

"I'm not quite sure yet, but this might have everything to do with it Jen. If Petr desperately needed other people's approval to feel better about himself, if he was willing to go to any length to get someone to like him, then I can see why that verse made him feel like he was trapped in an unending nightmare. I mean, think about it. If you've got to perform well to please others, and if their approval is where you get your sense of being OK with yourself, then that really is a nightmare. Jen, I know this will sound harsh, but the more I think about it the more I think Petr felt trapped in an unending nightmare because *he* put *himself* in the prison of needing to be liked by others. I mean, I remember all the way back to our Africa days; it was never enough for Petr. He was never satisfied with himself and with his own efforts — Petr had to have other people express their approval of him if he were to feel satisfied."

"Oh, Alfonso, that is exactly what it's still like! That is what it has always been like ever since I've known him. To be happy, he's always got to feel like someone else is happy with him. He's never satisfied with himself on his own merits. Oh, poor Petr. No wonder he's always so miserable!"

"Exactly, Jen. Because I know from first hand experience that living to make everyone in your congregation happy is a recipe for extreme frustration and bitterness. The more I piece together our recent conversations about this, Jen, the more I realize that Petr resented where life was taking him, and that is why he wanted out."

They were silent for a long time. Finally, Jennifer broke the silence and said, "Alfonso, there's something else even worse that Petr's been hiding from everyone lately, even from you."

What Is the Created Self?

We believe that at the core of Petr's misery and his inability to be resilient in the face of his trials is the fact that he ignored his "created self." This is the first leg of the three-legged stool of biblical differentiation.

The created self is the collection of a person's most essential, God-given qualities and characteristics. God created each individual with a unique set of strengths and weaknesses, abilities and liabilities, attractions and repulsions, and potentials and limits. All are deliberate gifts from God.

The created self includes a person's unique, special interests and preferences, as well as a person's non-negotiable values that cannot be violated without doing real damage to a person's sense of self. It includes a person's God-given strengths, talents and spiritual gifts. It is the seat of an individual's personality. Some might call it a person's very "soul." It has everything to do with a person's ability to be resilient when encountering trials.

In a noble but misguided attempt to "be all things to all people" (1 Cor. 9:19-23) Petr had suppressed his created self. He had misinterpreted Paul's phrase to mean that in order to be effective at ministry, pastors ought to ignore all their unique, God-given qualities and limits. This led him to do two dangerously destructive things: first, he squashed and ignored many of the special ways in which God had uniquely created him. Second, he failed to account for his weaknesses and vulnerabilities.

The Positive Side of Your Created Self

When Alfonso asked Jennifer about Petr's interests, like his motorcycle, certain books, and even jigsaw puzzles, we learned that Petr had put all those things on the backburner of life for the sake of success in ministry.

The cultivation of such interests is not identical with the cultivation of the created self. The created self is much broader and deeper than one's hobbies and preferences. But ignoring your preferences can be a significant sign that you are ignoring how God has uniquely created you.

In the 1980 movie *Chariots of Fire*, the main character, Eric Liddel, a devout Christian, must defend his participation in the Olympic Games to his sister who has religious qualms about it. She wonders if it is a betrayal of the Christian faith to perform in the Olympics. He tells her: "God made me for a purpose, for China [referring to his future missionary venture]... But He also made me fast. And when I run, I feel His pleasure. To give it up would be to hold Him in contempt." Liddel felt he would have been in rebellion against his created self if he refused to run. He felt he had been designed by God to run fast, and for him this was a key part of faithfully following Jesus. When he ran, he had a sense of the delight that the Godhead feels for His creation (Prov. 8:30-31). Anything less was to show "contempt" for His Creator.

If you are designed by God to do something well, part of your calling is to do it.

For example, if you practice a specific type of art, tinker with machines, care for animals, write computer code, play music, teach others a school subject, build homes, coach children in a sport, or cultivate a garden, then you are being true to your created self when you do those very things. In fact, it is part of following Jesus.

But if you are not doing those things that you were designed to do, you are being unfaithful to how God created you. It is even possible that you are in danger of showing contempt for your Creator.

If you're not convinced of the dignity, the worth and the value of your created self, or if you're not convinced that it figures so centrally into your life with God and your calling from Him, then it is time for you to re-visit the biblical proclamations of God's supreme approval and delight in all that He has made.

I'm sure we don't need to remind you of the *five times* Genesis 1 reiterates God's approval of His creation in general (vv. 4, 12, 18, 21, 25), and then His special approval ("*very* good") on the day He created humans (vs. 31). Much of this pleasure that God feels for His creation comes from how humanity displays His image (vs. 27). We know this because it was after our creation that He adds the "very" to "good."

This theme carries on throughout Scripture. For instance, Psalm 104, like many other passages in the Psalms, surveys all of creation like a low flying drone, taking into account all of its diversity and majesty and beauty. You feel God's exuberant happiness over His creation oozing out of every line of the Psalm. Then toward the end of this survey, verse 31 summarizes the wonder evoked by it all, saying "May the glory of the Lord endure for ever; *may the Lord rejoice in His works.*" God rejoices in His works because they glorify Him, if we follow the logic of the Psalm. His works show off His wisdom (vs. 24) and majesty (Ps. 19:1-2) and power (Isa. 40:26). Psalm 148, among many other Scripture passages, confirms this idea: "praise Him son and moon, praise Him all you shining stars … " (Ps. 148:3).

Or think of when God rebukes Job at the end of that book. God again surveys all of nature's wild power and diversity, and then right in the middle of it He slips in this statement: "all the angels shouted for joy" (vs. 7) when God "laid the earth's foundation" (vs. 4). Angels were shouting with joy when God created everything. His enjoyment of His creation infected all of heaven! How can we not join God in delighting in His creation? How can we not join His delight in our created selves, which were also designed to glorify Him (Isa. 43:7)?

Petr had been suppressing his created self by refusing to nurture any of his preferences, hobbies, or creative outlets. He made no room in his life to do the creative and recreational activities by which he might "feel God's pleasure." The fact that he had no room in his life for anything other than what is officially termed "ministry," is a telling sign that he had not been cultivating his created self.

You might object at this point and say that Petr was called to be a pastor, and that it is right for him to focus on fulfilling those duties. This is true, but God gave Petr additional interests, concerns and obligations that were not designed to be lost in favor of pastoring. Jesus was utterly focused on His calling and mission while on earth. But His mission not only involved the cross. The cross was certainly the climax of His calling, but every element of His incarnation, including his first thirty years in obscurity, were all parts of His calling. These years involved a childhood of playing and learning as well as a young adulthood of carpentry and business dealings.

By focusing on only one element of his calling, Petr leads an unbalanced life, out of sync with his created self. We often do the same, especially those of us who are ministers. We can tend to allow our created selves to drown in a sea of demands and expectations from other people.

You could rightly argue that ministry leadership requires a special focus that sometimes does not allow us to pursue all our desired interests. These can be luxuries that we don't always get to enjoy on the same level that others enjoy them. For instance, we must take to heart Paul's metaphor of the soldier, who refuses to "get entangled in civilian affairs" (2 Tim. 4:2). We must follow Paul's example of someone who refused to take advantage of any of the privileges of leadership, subverting them for the sake of the Gospel in order to be above reproach (1 Cor. 9: 15). He voluntarily limited himself in order to maximize his impact for the Gospel. When we pledge ourselves to be disciples of Jesus and ministers in His Name, we are saying that we are owned by Another, by One who determines our interests for us. Many private sacrifices of our good and legitimate preferences are involved in this focus.

And certainly, there are seasons of life, like studying in seminary, when you have to put some hobbies on the backburner. Other life seasons, like when your children are very young, demand that you sacrifice private luxuries for the benefit of others.

It is also true that some interests can threaten to take on a kind of idolatry in our hearts, and the only way to repent of the idolatry is by throwing out the interest entirely.

For instance, you have likely been prompted by God at one time or another to stop completely what would otherwise be an innocent and legitimate preoccupation. But it was irredeemably tinged with idolatry for you, so it had to be thrown away.

Furthermore, it is the case that not every interest lasts forever, but evolves over time according to our changing bodies, minds and relationships. Thus, you need not feel pangs of guilt for no longer desiring to do hobbies what once brought you pleasure as a teenager.

And it is important to say on this point that those with narcissistic tendencies (those who are self-absorbed and who see the world as revolving around them and their own interests) must be cautious when celebrating their preferences and interests. These are the people who are apt to take our book's message and respond with something like: "Great news! Now I know it's OK that I don't care if my wife and I haven't had a date in months. So what if she's starved for affection. I'm heading out to the golf course for 18 holes because it's what *I* want!" Those who struggle with narcissistic tendencies need to counteract those tendencies by using their gifts to serve the welfare of others, especially if they can do so without drawing attention to themselves.

However, even when we account for the special focus required of ministers, for unbalanced seasons like seminary, for the natural evolution of interests, or for the dangers of idolatry and narcissism, we are never called to narrow ourselves down permanently to a single task at the expense of all that brings us joy. These additional activities and interests express our unique design and enable us to contribute positively to the lives of other people. Embracing them, as part of following Jesus, makes us whole persons.

Failure to embrace them prevents our wholeness. Like Petr, this will leave us resentful of where life is taking us, because deep down we'll feel as if we are being unfairly denied some essential oxygen of life. If we feel forced to live life without any celebration of how God designed us, then no matter how noble the cause of our self-sacrifices, we will feel as if we've been kidnapped by life and forced to endure unending misery — misery without any relief.

Like Alfonso pointed out, this is "a recipe for extreme frustration and bitterness." If you interview pastors who've had affairs or been addicted to pornography, even though they knew it contradicted their faith and witness, you'll discover that it was this "unending nightmare" that made them feel pressured into immorality. Like Petr, they "want out," and immorality seemed to promise them this escape.

If you are a young pastor or church leader, you might not feel the immediacy of this danger. But the danger inevitably comes if you stick with ministry long enough. It can be counteracted by embracing your created self.

Have you embraced your created self, or does it lie bound up in a self-imposed prison?

The Dark Side of Your Created Self

Your strengths, talents and positive interests represent only one side of your created self. There is also the dark side of your created self and you need to take it into account.

When we say the "dark side," we are not talking here about Paul's idea of "the old self" (Col. 3:9) or the "sinful nature" (Rom. 7:18). The old self and the sinful nature are the part of a person that is intractably prone to resist God's lordship. This is the part of a person's heart, broken from the moment of the Fall, that is bound to fight against God. It is the part that automatically refuses to trust Him or submit to Him and instead turns to idols (Rom. 1:25).

The dark side we're talking about doesn't necessarily or automatically resist God, even though it can make it harder to obey God. Let us explain.

In Paul's point of view, the old self and the sinful nature describe the part of us that died when we were born again in Christ. This death does not mean that the old self disappears at conversion.

Rather, Paul told believers that we are to *consider* ourselves "dead" (Rom. 6:11) to this part of us that resists God. In other words, we are to treat it as dead and therefore we are never to feed or nurture it as we once did. Its ongoing influence in your life is to be continually resisted, by the grace and power of God. This old self pushes our behavior into sinful practices as a default whenever given the opportunity. These practices include, among many other things, failing to love others, sexual immorality and dishonesty. The old self is motivated by idolatry and self-love. God expects His followers to fight against it and to make progress in this fight, rendering the old self increasingly impotent.

By the "dark side" we mean the weaknesses and liabilities that are a natural part of being a human. It includes our tendencies to overdo bad things or underdo good things, our

gullibility in believing untruths, our susceptibility to cultivate unwarranted fears and
anxieties, our vulnerability to the negative
influences of others, our quickness to give in to
exhaustion when we ought to keep going, our
willingness to succumb to wrong desires, our
inability to maintain consistently good attitudes
and behaviors, our failure to remember
important truths, and our ineptitude at
restraining ourselves in the face of
overwhelming temptations.

All of these weaknesses can channel us
directly into real sin, but are not themselves sin.
Many of these kinds of shortcomings entered
our reality at the time of the original Fall, and to
that extent one can consider them derivative of
our total depravity. But they are not themselves
sin.

I (Andrew) once knew a Christian
minister I'll call "Jack," who failed to account for
and manage his tendency toward workaholism.
Jack's heart was in the right place and he eagerly
desired for all his efforts to go toward the
advance of the Gospel. And it is also true that
God had given Jack a daily dose of energy that
was remarkably well above average. So, Jack's
workaholism wasn't itself sin. But his good
intentions and abundant energy gave this
minister a blind spot, so that Jack couldn't tell
when he was about to hit the wall of his own
limits. He regularly found himself feeling

physically and emotionally depleted because he had ignored his limits. Jack eventually learned how to see his own blind spots and over time he gradually learned how to manage his work-aholism. Doing so wasn't like fighting sin because his tendency wasn't sin. Nevertheless, it hindered Jack's effectiveness until he learned to deal with it.

Some of our weaknesses have no moral component to them at all. These are things like forgetfulness, a physical disability, a difficulty managing money and time, or a sweet tooth. Again, some of these are indicative of the Fall because their origins can be traced to the Fall. But again, they are not themselves sin. While far less dangerous to our souls than the list of weaknesses we recounted above, this second list can also get us into trouble. Even the parts of our dark side that have no moral component still must be managed.

I (Andrew) was once acquainted with a Christian leader I'll call "Fred" who did not know how to manage his administrative weaknesses. He was an incredible visionary, but had little to no self-discipline or capacity for managing others in an efficient manner. Instead of accounting for this weakness by partnering with people with that strength, Fred had a very difficult time surrendering any bit of control. It would take too long to recount all the stories of how this hindered Fred's effectiveness.

Suffice it to say that Fred's leadership might have been so much more fruitful if he'd been willing to look at his blind spot with a greater degree of honesty and account for his weakness.

Every one of us has quite a lengthy list of weaknesses and vulnerabilities. This list is unique for every person. One person is susceptible to one danger while a second person is impervious to that same danger. However, that second person may be vulnerable to another danger that doesn't bother the first person in the slightest.

It is not only the kinds of weaknesses that vary from person to person — it is also the amount and degree of weaknesses that vary from person to person. Some individuals suffer from worse, more dramatic and more numerous weaknesses than others. These people experience a greater cost for failing to account for their dark side.

This is a hard truth to swallow in a society where most have been raised with democratic and egalitarian sensibilities, but we must be honest about it nevertheless.

There is absolutely nothing shameful about having weaknesses and limitations and liabilities, even severe ones, even ones that inconvenience and hurt others.

Jesus Himself had weaknesses, and He revealed them on occasion. For example, when He rested in the Samaritan town of Sychar, John described Him as "tired... from the journey" (John 4:6). Or, when He struggled in the Garden of Gethsemane to commit Himself entirely to God, Jesus revealed the human tendency to avoid hardship and self-sacrifice if possible.

For Jesus, these weaknesses were not in themselves sin, since Jesus was without sin (Heb. 4:15). They do demonstrate however that Jesus took on our frail humanity to the fullest extent possible.

God Himself purposefully designs our weaknesses and vulnerabilities. Therefore, we do not need to feel any shame about having them. They are part of our Creator's inbuilt means of feeling dependence on Him. But even though we need not be ashamed of them, we do need to account for them.

In other words, we need to manage them.

This is especially important because our dark side tends to nest right in the very shadow of our strengths. The dark side of an extrovert with strong social skills can be his overdependence on human approval.

Fred, mentioned above, was such an extreme extrovert that he couldn't sit still by himself long enough to work through a leadership problem—he had to interrupt co-workers from their work to process all his leadership difficulties (while still refusing to give up any control).

The dark side of an introvert with strong reflective and reasoning skills can be her self-absorption and morbid introspection. I (Andrew) know a Christian leader who is so extremely introverted that he can hardly make a public appearance. This prevents him from leading as effectively as he could.

The dark side of a strong leader can be a tendency toward authoritarianism. The dark side of a highly talented entertainer can be the propensity for drawing undue attention to himself. The dark side of an intellectually astute person can be her inclination to think of others as inferior.

A part of the responsibility of having a created self is to account for this dark side. Forgetful people account for this vulnerability by using more mnemonic devices to remind them of their duties. People with a tendency to gluttony compensate for it by avoiding situations with too much tempting food. People with a scarcity of energy manage it by planning ahead and by being very selective with how they use that limited energy. Those who lean toward pride, self-absorption and conceit must find ways to promote the welfare of others.

Petr Wolansky failed to account for a big part of his dark side: his tendency to crave human approval. Petr, much like King Saul described in the previous chapter, put great stock in whether people liked or disliked him. Gaining and keeping their approval was of enormous importance to him. He had even built his sense of being OK with himself around human approval.

Craving human approval by itself is not sin. Most self-described extroverts, for example, are highly motivated to be in the good graces of others. Countless actors and others who perform their duties report being motivated to do and improve their craft in order to please people. So this intuitive awareness of extroverts, of how others perceive them and how to adjust their behavior according to the perception of others, is an important gift that acts as a powerful social lubricant. But when a person fails to take into account the liabilities of this gift it becomes potentially dangerous, as it did in the case of King Saul and in Petr's case. It can devolve into idolatry.

Instead of structuring his life so that he could responsibly handle this vulnerability, Petr had designed his entire professional life to pursue human approval. He gave in to it every day, unabashedly. Making people happy had become his primary motive for leading and pastoring the church.

This weakness was the cause of his misinterpretation of 1 Corinthians 9:22. It was also the means of reinforcing the misinterpretation. Sometime in his early years as a Christian, Petr must have found this verse and thought he'd discovered a justification for this tendency to seek favor with people.

This misinterpretation was reinforced every time someone was "won over" by his charm, because it is easy to confuse peoples' approval of you with their true welfare. This confusion can occur even though it is clear from Scripture that human approval is not the same thing as the salvation for which Paul was willing to become "all things to all people."

And so Petr's neglect of his preferences and interests (the more positive side of his created self) worked in tandem with his failure to account for his dark side. Instead of resting confidently in the inherent goodness of whom God had created him to be, Petr had opted to ignore that part of himself. Instead of taking responsibility for his dark side, he gave in to it and nurtured it continually. His misinterpretation of the verse fed both tendencies and tied them together, motivating him to throw away the positive side of his created self in order to "be all things to all people," and encouraging him to make human approval his end goal, by means of those same words.

Instead of resulting in fruitfulness for God, all this led Petr to intense frustration and bitterness over his lot in life. It gave him a sense of being "trapped in an unending nightmare." He resented where life had taken him, and he wanted out.

How Does the Created Self Impact Leadership and Ministry?

If we understand our created self, we will have direction for how we are to live our lives and carry out our ministry assignments. But ignoring or neglecting one's created self can set a person up to fight vainly against her true nature. This is a recipe for bitter resentment toward God, toward others and toward life.

For instance, some ministers might have been created with strengths in the area of preaching, but they are quite limited in areas of administration. Ideally, they should craft their jobs around these created strengths and weaknesses. Ministers and their churches should work together to find ways in which their strength in preaching becomes a central part of their expected duties, and their weakness in administration is covered and accounted for in other ways.

But many leaders operate as if they are the exception to this rule. They feel they are above the need to pay attention to these strengths and weaknesses. They try to do it all, or they end up exploiting others to cover for their weaknesses. Other ministers, like Petr, misinterpret Paul's writing to mean that they must deny their every natural inclination for the sake of the ministry.

These ministry leaders inevitably end up resentful and bitter about their lot, often blaming their churches and family members for expecting them to do what they were never meant to do.

We argue that well-differentiated pastors know and embrace their uniquely created selves, and that they can confidently advocate to their churches that they ought to minister in ways that are most natural for their created selves. This is all part of nurturing and celebrating the positive side of the created self.

We also argue that well-differentiated pastors are in touch with the dark side of their created selves. They take responsibility for this dark side, and they do what it takes to manage it and reduce its potential for destruction.

This is what we mean by embracing the created self. On the one hand we are to understand, nurture and celebrate who God created us to be, with all our strengths, talents, giftings, contributions, preferences and special interests. At the same time, we are to understand and take responsibility for the dark side of our created self, allowing for the time, energy and forethought required to wisely manage it.

Chapter Three:
Embrace the Re-Created Self

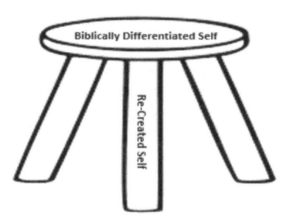

Biblically Differentiated Self

Re-Created Self

Alfonso, Petr and Jennifer

"What do you mean Jennifer?" asked Alfonso, with growing dread in his heart. "What do you mean by 'worse' than losing touch with his created self?"

"Well, I don't know what to call this struggle he had, but recently Petr confessed something to me that has really shaken me. It's kind of thrown into question everything we believe and everything we've built our lives on. And I think it might be at the root of his struggles."

"What do you mean Jen? Let's hear everything, now that we're psychoanalyzing Petr. I mean, what could it hurt now? We've got to put all our clues on the table."

"It's, well, I don't know how to say it exactly. It's that … I'm not totally sure that Petr has real faith in God?"

"How is that possible?" Alfonso instantly protested, maybe a little too harshly. "Petr has always been the most vocal about his faith of anyone I know. He felt called by God into ministry through all kinds of amazing signs. I was there for a bunch of them, so I remember. His faith in God has always been such an inspiration to me and to so many people. He's always been like a spiritual warrior for Jesus. I mean, I get that he's been going through a dark time in his faith recently, some sort of dark night of the soul or something. And I know he's been depressed, and I remember when I was depressed I didn't feel God at all. But, I mean, this is Petr we're talking about. I really don't get what you're trying to say Jen."

.

"No," Jen sighed with a deep weariness. "No, this isn't just depression and a 'dark night of the soul,' Alfonso. This is something different. It is so hard to explain…" Jen was groping for accurate words.

"Please try Jen. This probably does relate somehow. I mean, I still don't get how Petr wouldn't have 'real faith' like you say. His ministry has been so fruitful and effective and, and, well, powerful." Could Alfonso's image of Petr been based on a delusion?

"Well," Jen began, falteringly at first, "some of it has to do with how Petr believed that his worth was built on his ability to earn God's approval."

"Sorry, Jen," Alfonso interrupted, again a bit abruptly, "that just doesn't make any sense. Petr can preach the Gospel of God's unconditional acceptance better than anyone I know."

"No, no, he understood the Gospel, and he could preach it really well of course, but I'm talking about something different."

"Sorry I interrupted" Alfonso said.

"I mean, Petr confessed to me privately that deep down, way deep down, when it really mattered, he felt that his true worth as a human being was based on how good he could be for God. He told me that he knew this was a wrong belief — that he knew it contradicted the Gospel — but that he didn't know how to shake it."

Jen shook her head and went on, "He said that he could apply the Gospel of unmerited grace to the worst of sinners, but somehow, even after all that he's done for God, he's always struggled to apply it to himself."

"That is pretty disturbing," replied Alfonso. "But … I mean … I think all pastors go through seasons of being confused like that. But then, you know, God gives us fresh breakthroughs of grace."

"I know what you're talking about," said Jennifer. "I've seen others go through things like this, and so I asked Petr about that very thing. But he claimed never to have had a breakthrough like that, or that if he had, he couldn't remember it."

They both sat in silence for a long time. Alfonso didn't like this picture of his friend that was starting to come into focus. It was so different from the picture with which he was familiar.

"And there's more Al," Jen said after a while.

"Oh? Tell me more" Alfonso said unenthusiastically, not really wanting to hear it.

"Well, this wrong belief has something to do with another deep-down belief of his, that high quality results in ministry depend on his own efforts."

She paused for a moment to collect her words, "I can't tell you the number of times when, if something blocked him from getting ministry work done, Petr would get this desperate look in his eyes and say something to me like 'if I don't do this, then there's going to be no fruit!' Sometimes I challenged him on it, by saying 'what about God's grace? Doesn't the fruitfulness come from Him alone, not from our own efforts?' Petr would just get frustrated and say, all angrily, 'that doesn't apply. I've got to do my part or He won't do His.'"

"Hm. That approach would be a logical extension of thinking that your worth in God's eyes is based on your performance," Alfonso admitted.

"And another part of it, Alfonso, was that Petr started sounding more and more like how his mother used to talk about herself. I think it's related somehow."

"What do you mean Jen? I don't get it. His mother was quite a force of nature, I remember. But what are you talking about?"

"Well, I don't know if you ever spent enough time with Svetlana to hear her really get going on one of her tirades."

"Oh, I definitely heard her rants a lot. You couldn't spend more than 5 minutes with her before she started spouting her opinions about how 'all those ethnic minorities' were 'taking over' and how the 'Poles have endured more than anybody.'"

Alfonso rolled his eyes as he remembered.

"You know," he continued, "I can remember when she first found out that I, Petr's best friend from the mission field, was a Latino. She said something awful like, 'Petr, you're just supposed to minister *to* the natives, not *befriend* them!' I know, isn't that crazy? I was like, 'which century are we in?' It took her a long time to warm up to me and my brown skin, but I finally won her over by always bringing her favorite cookies," Alfonso said with a wry smile and a shake of the head.

Both Alfonso and Jen broke the tension with a laugh about Petr's domineering and opinionated mother, Svetlana Wolansky. Memories of funny stories of her inappropriate comments came back to them both, momentarily alleviating the seriousness of the situation.

"Oh, Svetlana," Jen said shaking her head. "That woman almost killed me with her controlling ways and her racism and all her emotional baggage. But I'm not talking about that part of her so much. After you spent *a lot* of time with her, like I did, it slowly came out that deep down, she believed in her heart of hearts that she was a victim of life."

"Svetlana? A victim? No way," Alfonso said in disbelief. "That woman survived so much tough stuff. Escaping communist-controlled Poland, all on her own? Making her way in America without any English at first? Raising Petr as a single mom, all on the income from a house-cleaning job and from a factory night shift? I mean, my mom was a house cleaner too, but we also had my dad's income from his roofing business. No, Svetlana was no victim. She was a hardscrabble survivor if ever I saw one, and she was as tough as nails, that woman was. I mean, I hated her racism, but I sure respected her for overcoming so many challenges."

"Yes, I respected her for all that too, Al. But I don't mean that," Jennifer responded. "I mean, when you really let her get going (which I did more and more in her last years because I discovered that was the only way to have a peaceful relationship with her), she would start to say that she was still bitter about all those hardships she'd faced. She resented them. And she resented her life more and more as life went on."

"Hmm, interesting."

"And I remember this one time when our little John, I think he was just like four or something, asked her straight up: 'Gama, why are you so angry at life? Didn't Jesus help you? Didn't He make it all better fo' you?' You know, how little kids will just speak up and say the truth, without any fear. And I'll never forget how she responded: 'Oh, you'll see Johnny. We're all victims of God's wrath.' Boy, I remember having to talk John through the confusion of that statement."

"I guess that does kind of fit with how I remember her," Alfonso admitted.

Jennifer went on: "You know how some old people who are so close to Jesus just get sweeter as they age? Their life's trials actually soften and sweeten them? Well, it was just the opposite with Svetlana. It was like her heart hardened and she just grew more bitter. And she'd rehearse her trials to herself, as her body was less and less able to stay busy. And that just made her angrier and angrier. She got angrier at life, and angrier at God. I think that anger was why she didn't mind Petr converting to Protestant evangelicalism, despite his Catholic upbringing. In her mind, his conversion was kind of a fist of protest against a God that she saw as harsh and unmerciful."

"I do hope she's resting in peace now," Alfonso said. "I mean, I believe she did confess Jesus as Lord at one point, near the end. But what does this have to do with Petr now?"

"Well, the thing is, I've been hearing Petr say things in the last few years that sound so much like Svetlana. He doesn't use the exact same words, but they're things that make me think he sees himself as a victim too, like she saw herself. For example, about a year ago we were struggling with this credit card debt. In the middle of that, I reminded him of how we'd survived that foreclosure ordeal a few years before that."

"Oh yeah, that was terrible. I remember," Alfonso acknowledged.

"And I said to him, 'If God got us through the foreclosure, can't we trust Him to get us through this trial?' But Petr exploded, just like his mother used to, and started going off on this rant about how that foreclosure episode was just more evidence that God was out to get us."

"But I thought everything ended well with the foreclosure thing? Didn't the bank let you restructure the mortgage and they even forgave a bunch of it?"

"That's what I was trying to remind him of! But instead Petr's overarching memory of the whole incident was how God's out to get us. It's like he's adopted as his own his mother's interpretation of life that he is, at his core, this persecuted victim."

"Huh," said Alfonso. "So, first, Petr believes that his worth is built on his ability to earn God's approval. Second, he believes that high quality results in ministry depend on his own efforts. And third, he has adopted as his own his mother's self-narrative that he is a persecuted victim?"

"That exactly sums it up Alfonso," Jennifer said grimly.

"So, what we're looking at is that Petr has failed to apply critical aspects of his re-created self to his deepest sense of identity."

"Whoa, English please Al. You're not delivering a lecture to a conference of egg-heads."

80

"Sorry," Alfonso apologized. "What I mean is that instead of accepting and believing in his new identity in Christ, Petr has continued to live according to his old identity apart from Christ. I work with parishioners all the time who have this same struggle. It's really common, even among pastors. It's just hard for me to accept that all this time Petr has had the same struggle. Maybe because he's such a good friend I couldn't see it as clearly?"

"The problem," Jennifer went on, "is that it makes me question the authenticity of Petr's faith in the first place. And if we don't even have that foundation, how do I know if God's even hearing his prayers? I mean, what if he's successful at taking his life, Al? What if he dies and he doesn't even know God, and..." She trailed off as fresh tears welled up in her eyes.

"Jen," Alfonso jumped in, kicking fully into pastoral mode now, "God is a God of grace. He's not expecting Petr to reach some point of perfectly understanding it all before hearing his prayers. Besides, having this struggle doesn't mean Petr wasn't a real Christian. All I said was that Petr is having a hard time *applying* the message of God's grace."

Jen nodded silently, but the tears kept coming.

Alfonso continued, sounding calm and unemotional for the first time. "You know Jen, it makes more sense to me now why Petr's such a perfectionist and such a workaholic who can never rest from ministry. I mean, I used to think he was just a high-energy guy who was a little too addicted to the adrenaline of ministry. But what you're saying makes more sense of this need he's always had to be several steps ahead of God, as if that were even possible. People who struggle to apply their re-created identity to themselves often are workaholics. It's like they're desperate to prove something. I've seen it so many times.

"And," he went on, "I'm finally understanding now why Petr tended to feel sorry for himself whenever he encountered trials, and why he tended to blame others for these trials. I remember seeing it way back when we were in Africa, and I just assumed it was a maturity thing; that he would grow out of it. But you know Jen, it makes sense to me more than ever now why Petr felt so exhausted, so burned out, and so ready to throw in the towel, not just on ministry but on life."

His last statement caused another flood of tears from Jennifer, who put her head in her hands. Alfonso realized that his detached, clinical sounding speculations had been insensitive, and not what Jen needed to hear at this time. He was supposed to be here to offer Jennifer emotional support. He put an arm around her.

After some awkward throat clearing, Alfonso stood up and absent-mindedly poured himself more coffee, forgetting again how unacceptably weak it was until he took another sip and it was too late. Choking it down he asked, "Where's this all getting us anyways?" He crossed the room again and began leafing through Petr's journal.

After skimming through several pages Alfonso stopped and took an interest in one entry in particular. He re-read it a couple of times, then said "Jen, I think I found something else important. Listen to this..."

Applying the Re-Created Self

We argue that the second leg on which biblically differentiated people rest is their new nature in Christ, the *re-created self*. Ministers who hope to be resilient when facing life's inevitable trials must build their sense of self on Scriptural truths about their identities. They must look to how the Bible re-defines them instead of how their culture and upbringing define them.

Plenty of good Christian books have been written, especially in the last 30-40 years, which thoroughly outline our new identity in Christ.

You could probably rattle off quite a number of the elements of this new identity without much help from us. You might even be thinking, "I'll just skip this chapter—it's too basic." But given how so many seasoned, experienced pastors and church leaders fail to apply the truths of their new identity, isn't it worth a deeper look at the issue?

It is fairly self evident, especially to those of us in ministry, that our actions are powerfully shaped by our beliefs about our identities. A seasoned pastor friend of ours, "Frank," tells a story that illustrates this point. He is a Caucasian man who grew up in the southern Mexican state of Oaxaca. He is the child of Caucasian missionaries from North America.

Like anybody growing up, Frank desired to fit in to his surroundings. So, he made it his goal early on to adopt Mexican cultural behaviors and to do them as well as or even better than his Mexican neighbors. For instance, he made sure to learn how to speak Spanish as well as or even better than his neighbors. His cultivated a perfect accent that was utterly indistinguishable from that of a native speaker.

Frank strove in school to make sure his Spanish grammar, syntax and spelling were above reproach, in case anyone ever accused him of not knowing Spanish as well as native speakers. And because he often worked outside to help his parents in their missionary work, he had become tan in a way that made his skin even darker than many of his Mexican neighbors. He hoped from this that no one would be able to call him "white." All he had to do to refute them was point to his skin.

But despite all these efforts, Frank could not overcome the fact that with blond hair, blue eyes, a stature well over six and a half feet in height, and classic Scandinavian features, he would never be seen as fully Mexican.

This pastor tells a funny story of how this effort to make his identity into something it was not caught up with him one time. One day as a young man he took a group of visiting North American relatives to relax at a local beach. This particular beach charged money for people to enjoy it, and there were two prices, one for native Mexicans and one for foreign tourists. Not surprisingly, tourists were charged more than Mexicans. Frank, hoping to get his relatives a deal, spoke with the person collecting money, in perfect Spanish, saying that these relatives were with him and therefore ought to be charged the lower price for Mexicans. He'd seen this work plenty of times at other tourist sites when Mexicans helped non-native friends get the lower native prices. But the money collector took one look at Frank and demanded the tourist price instead. The two began a heated argument about the price.

During the whole argument, Frank kept thinking to himself "But I'm *from* here! Why can't this person see that?! *I am Mexican!*" He grew more and more furious as the money collector refused to budge on the price.

Frank's relatives were happy to pay the higher tourist price, and they kept telling him that they would do so. But the argument continued as Frank grew increasingly horrified at the injustice of being treated as if he were any other gringo. It went on until Frank's exasperated relatives finally insisted on paying the full tourist price. For the rest of the day, an incensed Frank grumbled indignantly to himself over the incompetence of this beach official for being unable to recognize his obvious Mexican identity. It was a painful eye-opener that, no matter how Mexican Frank *felt*, he would never be accepted as anything but a gringo.

Frank, now ministering in the United States, looks back on this story and pokes fun at his case of mistaken identity with a wry sense of humor. But it illustrates the need for Christians to get right their new identity in Christ.

The story shows what an enormous influence our *sense* of identity exerts on our behavior and on our overall well-being. Frank's childhood obsession with perfecting the Spanish language and Mexican customs was driven by a sense of identity. Countless hours of his childhood were spent pursuing his simplistic view of identity. It was hard for Frank the accept the more complex identity of being a North American of European descent raised in Mexico. It took some time and some hard experiences for Pastor Frank's *sense* of identity to catch up with the more complicated reality. In the meantime, he suffered in these rough encounters more than he needed to.

The story also shows the place identity has in our ability to be resilient. If Frank had been able to be more clear-headed in those years about his complex identity as an American-Mexican, he might have been more resilient in the face of that particular disappointment. He could have soothed himself more effectively in the moment by reminding himself: "Yes, this person is acting unjustly, but how could he do anything else, given my confusing appearance? As frustrating as this is, I know that nothing has been taken away from me in any true sense." Instead, a big part of Frank's frustration was the feeling, however naïve, that something in the very core of his identity was being violated. It is very difficult to recover from violations of identity, perceived or real.

Frank did happen to recover quickly in this case, but he would have preferred to be a calm and loving Christian witness instead of fuming and resentful that day. He would have liked to be a "non-anxious presence," in Murray Bowen's language, for the sake of his own sense of peace and composure, not to mention for the sake of his Christian witness. Instead, the mistaken identity had left him in a tailspin of confusion and overpowering emotions for a moment.

So many Christian leaders experience similar emotional tailspins because they find it hard to be clear-headed about their new identities in Christ in the face of disappointments, setbacks, and trials. Even if they know the facts of their new Christian identity, as Frank did, many don't know how to apply those facts when confronted with troubling realities.

Frank's personal struggle over his identity helped him effectively minister years later when he was the youth pastor of a thriving, small town church in the Upper Midwest. He was able to relate deeply to the many young people who were going through their own identity struggles. It is extremely normal for teenagers and young adults to wrestle over their identities. But some wrestle more than others. This was true of one young man, who we will call John, for whose sake Frank's earlier struggles had prepared him perfectly.

John was a member of Frank's youth group. Like Frank, he was also obviously Caucasian, and had been raised in this small Upper Midwestern town by his biological, Caucasian parents. But he had gradually accepted a bizarre lie about himself that he was in fact native Mexican. Frank was never sure exactly where this young man first got this idea into his head. But over time John had concocted a story that his parents had kidnapped him from a Mexican orphanage as an infant and had attempted to hide this truth from him. John wholeheartedly pursued a Mexican identity, in spite of his parents' insistence to the contrary. He thoroughly cloaked himself in this Mexican identity. Even more bizarrely, he was able to teach himself perfect Spanish in an unbelievably short time period. John fully believed his own delusional story that he was Mexican. He started to have an odd, glassy appearance in his eyes and increasingly became almost catatonic when addressed in English.

John's family was bewildered. Why had their beloved son succumbed so fully to this strange web of lies? They were heartbroken to see him move further and further into a fantasy and away from a sense of reality about his identity. Furthermore, his ability to speak perfect Spanish so suddenly had piqued their concern that perhaps there was some sort demonic activity involved.

John's parents came to Pastor Frank in desperation. The three of them committed to pray and fast together for a period of time, asking God to rescue John from the self-deception and from any possible demonic influence. In the following days, they hatched a strategy to help John confront the truth.

After several days of intense struggle in prayer for John, Pastor Frank and John's parents sat down with him and directly confronted him about the lies he had believed. They staged it a little bit like when caring relatives hold an intervention for a loved one who struggles with addiction. At first, John resisted any effort to disabuse him of his delusion. But finally, his parents pulled out his birth certificate and said "John, unless this piece of paper was forged, you were born right here in the United States and have no Mexican heritage at all. We remember the moment you were born, and we haven't taken our eyes off you for a moment since." When John saw the birth certificate, something inside him changed. He broke down crying and admitted he had believed a lie about himself. Instantly, the glossy appearance in his eyes evaporated, and John forgot how to speak perfect Spanish.

This true story is admittedly very unusual. But what isn't unusual is the similar confusion many Christians feel about their true identity. Christians often base their sense of identity around more non-biblical stories than biblical ones.

Like John, many *feel* these non-biblical identities to be more real than the biblical ones. Sadly, this cannot simply be credited to ignorance. Even when they have been adequately educated about their identity in Christ, many fail to hold on to their new identity because they have failed to cherish it for the precious reality that it is. Rather than seeing it as a treasure of unspeakably great value, many have discarded it as easily as John discarded his identity as the beloved child of his parents. As with John, something in the false identity offered by the world presents itself as more alluring than the truth that is in Christ.

Even sadder is the fact that plenty of Christian leaders and pastors have a similar confusion about their new identity as Christians. Many cherish their precious identity in Christ no more than nominal Christians who live mostly in the world's delusions about self.

We can all recall moments when, like Frank, we behaved badly and felt miserable because we had lost touch with our re-created self in Christ. Some of us can remember seasons when, like John, we were positively lost because we had drifted from our new identity in Christ and had replaced it with the identity offered to us and enforced in us by the world. Think through any past situations in which you can relate to this. Think of how such identity confusion led to difficulties and failures to be resilient.

Petr Wolansky had clearly lost track of his re-created self in Christ. Instead, he had adopted and bought into lies that his worth was built on his ability to earn God's approval. He believed that high quality results in ministry depend on his own efforts. And he had adopted as his own his mother's self-narrative that he was at his core a persecuted victim. What terrible burdens for anyone to bear.

Is it any wonder that Petr felt strained past the point of breaking? Is it any wonder that, despite all his gifts and strengths, Petr felt too frail to go on?

But when ministers base their life and ministry on their re-created self in Christ, they discover a new freedom because they now see God's love (for themselves and for others) as the motivation for ministry activity. They can see the fruit of ministry to be the result of God's intentional kindness rather than the result of their own efforts. Rather than a harsh taskmaster who expects productivity or else, God now appears as the unendingly generous Source of everything good, as One who delights to give with lavishness the heart's desires of His children (Luke 11:5-8, Rom. 8:32, Eph. 1:8, 1 John 3:1). Ministers who apply these truths deeply to their understanding of God and of themselves come to experience them as realities instead of just sweet-sounding platitudes.

Consider how it might affect the way you do ministry to base your identity more squarely on your re-created self. For instance, imagine how it might influence your ministry and leadership if you more deeply treasured the truth that you are an unconditionally beloved and approved of child of God (1 John 3:1) and an object of God's unilaterally granted, unmerited favor (Rom. 5:8).

We know you've learned, studied and perhaps even preached on these truths before. But take a moment right now to meditate on them. Savor them and let your imagination soar about how life could be different if they were real.

Think of the internal rest you might enjoy knowing that these truths meant you had direct and privileged access to your heavenly Papa's ear (Ps. 6:9, 116:1), and therefore you could expect to be heard and answered by the God who bears all your personal and ministry burdens?

Think of the internal rest you might enjoy if you these truths meant your ministry success flowed from His generosity and not your efforts.

Think of how your spirit might relax knowing that your fruit bearing (John 15:1-5), the productivity Jesus demands of us as His disciples (John 15:16), flowed not from your anxious intensity, self-sacrifices and concentration on your goals, but simply from God's zeal for His own glory to accomplish His work (Isaiah 9:7, 48:7).

Or, imagine how it might influence your ministry and leadership if you more deeply absorbed the Scriptural view of God as all loving and sovereign, the One who does all things for your greatest good, for the greatest of good of those you lead (Rom. 8:28-37) and for His own glory (Isaiah 43:7). What a burden might be lifted from your heart if you could consistently regard these truths as a reality, in the very face of contrary winds. How your trials would gain a note of purpose and even victory if you could hold on to these truths.

Most evangelical, orthodox ministers start out in ministry agreeing to these beliefs. In fact, these beliefs are often the original inspiration for pursuing a career in ministry. When their significance first dawns on us, we feel compelled to communicate them and lead others to embrace them. How can we not commit our lives to doing so, in light of the transforming power of these truths?

But the reality is, many of us fail to cultivate and deepen our embrace of these truths, especially after ministry starts to get hard. Many of us fail to do the ongoing and tedious work, after the early flush of ministry success fades, of pressing these doctrines more thoroughly into the fabric of our being, internally sorting out how these truths apply to us and to our ministry efforts.

Ongoing application gets difficult when ministry begins to lose its initial luster. After the honeymoon period of ministry is over and obvious fruit can feel like a rare occurrence, many fail to keep pushing for the applications of these truths. What does it mean that God "predestined us for adoption to sonship through Jesus Christ, in accordance with His pleasure and will" (Eph. 1:5) when it's been years since you've seen visible fruit in your ministry, when your marriage is strained to the breaking point, and you can't recall a time that you tasted joy in ministry? You sure don't feel like a predestined and privileged son or daughter in these stretches of little apparent fruit.

What does it mean that you were "predestined … in order that [you] might be for the praise of His glory" (Eph. 1:11-12) when you can't point to one concrete thing you've done in the last year, despite all your busyness, which you know resulted in the praise of God's glory?

What does it mean to be a beloved child of God when people's compliments of your sermons become less and less frequent, when you run up against more resistance than support, and when you realize that peoples' earlier efforts to encourage you were out of pity for your newbie status and not because they actually liked or endorsed you?

At this point, a lot of ministers stop short with only superficial applications of biblical truths about their new identities in Christ. Instead of seeing the endlessly disappearing horizon of application, they secretly suspect these supposed "truths" were only an inch deep after all. At this point, it is common for cynicism toward God's truth to creep in to the hearts of even the most devout ministers.

But if you really consider the biblical truths about your identity, what end is there to applying the simple truth that God loves you (Rom. 5:8) when His love is, by definition, infinite in its dimensions? Even so, it gets hard to treasure these truths, through the setbacks, all the way to the point in which they become a lived reality.

It is important to consider that many of the biblical characters who persevered, who "we count as blessed" (James 5:11), who ended up experiencing God's rewards, did so because God required them to apply the truth about their identities and about God when they were in the harshest conditions possible. We're sure at least a dozen or so examples of this from Scripture spring instantly to your mind. Glance through Hebrews 11 to jog your memory.

But ministers who fail to deepen their application of biblical truths about their re-created selves threaten to cut themselves off from God's love.

We're not talking here about the old red herring of "losing one's salvation." We're talking about our failure to draw upon the power and grace and wisdom and inspiration of God and apply it to ministry and to ourselves. This failure can be a set up for burn out and for a big crash. Jesus never intended humans to run on the fuel of their own efforts and passion, but on the fuel of God's love and God's glory.

It's no wonder that many burn out of ministry after losing touch with their re-created selves.

Petr, despite all his ministry training, years of successful ministry work, and giftedness, had not deeply applied all the truths of his re-created self to his identity in thorough and transformative ways. Instead of accepting and believing in his new identity in Christ, Petr continued to live according to his old identity apart from Christ. Let's look at how Petr neglected to embrace his re-created self.

First, Petr believed that his worth was dependent on his ability to earn God's approval. This is a sign that at the very core of his being, Petr had not absorbed and treasured the truth that he was worthwhile and significant simply because God loved him and for no other reason. The whole narrative of Scripture, beginning with the very first chapter in Genesis, paints a picture of humanity as the crowning achievement of God's creation and the object of His unearned pleasure and love. God has always conferred dignity and worth on us unilaterally, without any initiation from our side. His condemnations in Scripture of human misbehavior and misbelief results from His prior held love for us, not His disdain for us. His wrath is in reality the exasperation and broken heart of a parent who is overly in love with his wayward children. The unlimited approval and pleasure that the Father takes in the Son (Matt. 3:17) is applied to all who are in Christ through their faith in Him.

Second, Petr believed that high quality results in ministry depended on his own efforts. This contradicts what both Jesus and Paul carefully explained on numerous occasions. In John's Gospel, Jesus defines discipleship as "bearing fruit" (John 15:8), saying that fruit is the proof of the authenticity of one's discipleship. But this definition is embedded in Jesus' metaphor of the True Vine and the branches. He explains how "no branch can bear fruit by itself; it must remain in the vine." He paints this picture in which fruit bearing is totally dependent on the Vine. Then He says to His disciples: "Neither can you bear fruit unless you remain in me." So, the anxiety a would-be disciple might feel over Jesus' demand to bear fruit is resolved by His promise to provide everything to bear that fruit. Jesus here promises to be the source of the fruit He demands.

But Petr, instead of looking to Jesus, the True Vine, as the source of all the fruit demanded of him, looked to his own efforts, his own ingenuity, his own charm, to accomplish things for God. This creates at least two problems. First, it leads to a sense of burn out. After all, who wouldn't feel burned out after believing themselves responsible to achieve results that are as high quality as what God achieves? The task is just too impossibly demanding. Second, it leads to a sense of resentment toward God, resentment for burdening the disciple instead of shouldering those burdens for the disciple. Jesus promises to bear our burdens and He invites us to share His yoke rather than the world's yoke (Matt. 11:28-30). But who would not be resentful toward a God who gave burdens instead of relieved them?

Paul also makes it clear that fruitfulness comes from God alone. The most obvious passage on this theme is his discussion of the "fruit of the spirit" in his letter to the Galatians (5:22-23). It is instructive to notice that Paul did not intend this list to be memorized out of context, like most of us have our children do in our children's ministries. Rather, it is one link in a chain of an argument. His argument is to persuade the Galatians to trust in God's grace rather than their own efforts (2:16, 3:2-6, 3:11). By the time he arrives at the list of fruit, he has already established the human inability to gain God's favor through our own effort. He has just explained that the practice of serving one another in love (5:13) comes out of the freedom of trusting God's grace.

Third, Petr had adopted as his own his mother's self-narrative that he was a persecuted victim. This belief logically follows the first two beliefs. After all, if you do not believe that you are an object of God's unilateral, unearned affections, how else do you comfort yourself throughout life's hardships? Seeing yourself as a victim can suffice for a temporary and shallow kind of comfort if you don't really believe the biblical truth about yourself. And if you believe that your fruitfulness comes from your own effort, how else do you explain your ministry failures if you've been trying your hardest? Seeing yourself as a victim does a good job of explaining the source of your failures when, as far as you can tell, you've done all you can to ensure success. Petr's belief in his victimhood also naturally flowed from his upbringing. If he had been soaking in his mother's victimhood his whole life, it would be hard to blaze a new trail of identity that departed from his origins.

This does not mean that victimization was entirely and only in the imaginations of Petr and his mother Svetlana. It is quite possible that they really were victimized at times, especially given Svetlana's upbringing in a repressive country.

Real victimization occurs to all kinds of people, all the time. But a victim *mentality* is different than real victimization. This mentality is a lens through which one interprets all of life's events. It trains you to see yourself as a victim, even when no actual victimization has taken place.

One problem with seeing yourself as a victim is that it removes much of the inner strength it takes to be resilient in trials. A person with a victim mentality tends to feel the hurt of a past victimization for a long time after it has already occurred. This can have a debilitating effect on your present capacity, since much of your current energy must go to nursing the old wounds.

A victim also tends to interpret daily events as more victimization. Events that others might shrug off as the normal wear and tear of the daily grind can feel like personal attacks if you have a victim mentality.

Worse yet, those with a victim mentality tend to expect more victimization. So even if one event works out well, another violation or grievance is sure to be just around the corner. It is similar to how many trauma survivors cringe and wince as they walk through life. They do this because they anticipate re-traumatization. It is an understandable survival mechanism. A traumatized person goes through life wondering (and therefor living in the fear of), another trauma exploding into his or her reality with no warning. Many traumatized people believe that if they anticipate this next trauma, they might be able to minimize its impact, whether or not this belief is based on logic.

Likewise, a person with a victim mentality goes through life cringing and wincing in expectation of more victimization. The original victimization may have legitimately occurred, but for someone with a victim mentality, the first victimizing event illogically means that another could happen at any time, with no warning. This leaves a person on edge and tends to demolish any energy that he might otherwise have to face current challenges.

But Scripture is clear that God's followers are not victims, at least not as part of their permanent identity. Paul writes: "in all these things we are more than conquerors through him who loves us" (Rom. 8:37). This statement is part of the climax of his argument throughout the whole letter to the Romans, in which he is trying to persuade his readers of their new identity in Christ. He builds up to this statement by explaining how God sees the trials and suffering of the Roman Christians. He writes: "I consider that our own present sufferings are not worth comparing with the glory that will be revealed in us..." (vs. 18) because, "in all things God works for the good of those who love Him, who have been called according to His purpose" (vs. 28).

Paul then tackles perhaps the greatest lie people believe when suffering: that somehow the suffering means that our most important treasure of all, God's own love, is being taken away from us. But the truth is that neither "trouble, or hardship or persecution or famine or nakedness or danger or sword … death nor life … angels nor demons … present nor the future … any powers … height nor depth, nor anything else in all creation, will be able to separate us from the love of God that is in Christ Jesus our Lord" (vs. 35 and 38-39).

Paul uses the most extreme hyperbole imaginable to convince his listeners that their worst trials will not end in the loss of their greatest treasure, God's love.

Sadly, those with a victim mentality cut themselves off from this kind of victor's mentality described by Paul. Petr and his mother cut themselves off from benefiting from the truth in Paul's arguments. No wonder suicide felt like a better option than living. If you have taken as gospel truth the belief that you are, at the heart of everything, a victim, then it is logical to despair of life. It won't ever get any better than it is now for someone whose identity is "permanent victim."

The way to address some of Petr's issues is to apply the Scriptural truths that reveal one's re-created self, or one's new identity in Christ. The appendix at the back of this book highlights just a few of these Scriptural truths. You probably have access to a much more extensive list, and this one suffers from phrases being taken out of context. But it is an adequate place to re-launch your efforts to apply these truths to your heart and mind.

Chapter Four:
Embrace the Self-in-Relation with the Creator and Created

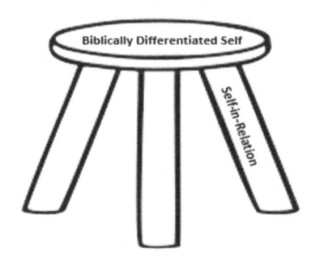

Biblically Differentiated Self

Self-in-Relation

Alfonso, Petr and Jennifer

"I don't think I can handle many more negative revelations," Jennifer said, her voice sounding dull and withdrawn now. "What is it?"

"Well, I'm sort of wondering now if you were right Jen, about Petr's faith. Listen to this:

> *I can't take any more of this faking it crap. I feel like such an imposter. I am so hollow right now. Why does the hollowness have to keep coming back, even after I've made someone happy? I can strongly exhort anyone in the church to seek God and to trust and obey Him. But I just personally feel nothing. I've gotten all this feedback lately that my sermons have sparked real faith in people. But I feel so hollow when I give the sermons, like there's no real faith in me. It seems like I get more life from studying ancient Greek and all those stupid early church controversies than from actually relating to God. I'm pretty sure He doesn't even listen to me anyways. I am so trapped in this unending nightmare.*

"See!" blurted Jennifer. "It's just like I was telling you! No real faith! And that word he keeps using, 'hollow.'"

"Well, this is a little different, Jen," replied Alfonso calmly. "We were just talking about Petr's beliefs about himself and about God. This is more about his *relationship* with God."

"Alfonso, I'm too exhausted for this hair splitting. I swear, that is all you theologians do sometimes. Not helpful."

"No, no, I'm not just splitting hairs Jen. And I think this might give us some kind of clue to where he is, so humor me a bit, OK? Just listen."

"OK," said Jennifer wearily. "What's this O-so-important distinction you're making?"

"So, this entry, and a few of the others I'm reading, talk about Petr's direct relationship with God, right? They express how he interacted with God, not just what he believed about himself and God. I mean, the two things are related of course, but they're not identical. But he keeps using this word 'hollow' to describe how he feels about himself and God."

"Yeah, like I was saying earlier. It's just like the other word he keeps using, 'empty.' Go on."

"Well, listen to this other entry," Alfonso urged:

*I finally got that old bag in the 3rd row
to smile at my joke in the sermon
yesterday! I think that's a first! I think
I'm really close to winning over her
and those old bats she hangs out with.
They are so critical of everything. But
no one can withstand the charms of
Old Mr. Sweet Smile for very long. I'll
soon win them over, and then Mr.
Sweet Smile won't feel so hollow
anymore.*

"Hmm. There's that word again, 'hollow.'"

For the first time that morning, Jennifer actually broke out into a sincere laugh: "Ah, I know exactly who that 'old bag' is he's talking about. She really is a cranky old lady. I actually remember that day he's talking about in the journal. And that sounds exactly like Petr, always wanting to win everyone over with that charm of his," she was smiling pleasantly at the memories. "And why am I not surprised that he uses that silly nick name in his own journal!? I thought that was just a pet name between the two of us. Geeze, what a narcissist." Jennifer continued to chuckle to herself.

"I think 'narcissist' is going a bit too far. I've dealt with a few of those, and Petr wasn't that. But I do know how charming he can be. I remember so many times I saw him turn on the charm to smooth his way through tough situations." Alfonso chuckled to himself as well, remembering a few of Petr's escapades over the years.

"Like I said, I think that's why it's killing him that he can't win over the board chair," Jennifer observed.

"Exactly. And I actually think that that fact and these entries have a lot in common," Alfonso interjected.

Jennifer looked at him quizzically.

"Listen to this one from just a few weeks ago, and then I'll explain," Alfonso said:

Since God won't have anything
to do with me, at least I can die
knowing how many people thought I
was important. God won't miss me of
course when I end it all, but at least I
can be assured that certain people will
miss me. I've worked so hard to win
over this congregation and to make it
successful. I'm in their hearts. Man,
are they ever going to be sorry about
losing me. I may not make it to heaven,
but at least I'll be stuck in their
imaginations forever. And they will be
sorry. At least I won't feel hollow
anymore. At least I'll wake up from
this unending nightmare.

The mention of not making it to heaven instantly brought Jennifer out of her reverie. When Alfonso saw tears welling up in her eyes again, he quickly stopped and launched into his explanation.

"Jen, I'm getting at something important here, which might be a clue. See, there's this pattern of relating to God, this sense that he's 'hollow' in his faith. In recent years he's neglected intimacy with Him. God is this angry *thing* to him, distant and uncaring. It seems Petr's been outright ignoring Him because of that perception. I'm not trying to dishonor Petr. I'm just trying to say it like it is. I mean, we kind of have to shatter all illusions here Jen if we're going to get to the bottom of this. Know what I mean?"

Jen stared mutely at the floor but nodded in agreement.

"So," continued Alfonso, "I'm horrified at the idea that my best friend pulled the wool over my eyes about his relationship with God, at least recently. But, no matter how close he used to feel to God, we have to face the fact that of late, his faith life has been a hollow shell. You heard him use the word himself, 'hollow.' I'm not happy about it, but it's a fact."

After a pause Alfonso sipped more unpleasant coffee and then swallowed it down with a grimace. He went on: "And that's where I see the connection to the second passage, Jen. I know it's kind of funny that he called this lady in your church an 'old bag,' but did you hear the way he sort of de-humanized her? Made her out to be a *thing*? Thought of her as a project?"

Jennifer broke in, defensive now, "Alfonso, that is a mean thing to say. Petr is so dedicated to the people in our church. He'd do anything to make them happy. He was trying to make that old lady laugh, which, let me tell you, she really needs to do. All the years I've been there, I seriously think I can count on one hand the number times I've seen her even smile."

"Jen, you agreed that we're going to be brutally honest here. It's the only way we're going to make progress. No more illusions about Petr, OK? And again, I'm not trying to denigrate him. This is eating me up Jen, to talk about someone I love. But we've got to get rid of all illusions at this point."

"Well, you kind of sound like you are trying to denigrate him, Al."

"Brutal honesty Jen. We agreed. OK?"

"Just finish what you were trying to say," she said, the defensive tone still dominating her voice.

"Let's get real Jen. Was he really trying to make that woman laugh for *her* sake, for *her* happiness? Or was he trying to get her to laugh for *his* sake? I mean, listen to this again." He re-read the second entry out loud. "I think Petr was trying to win her over for *his own* sense of significance. His jokes served himself, Jen."

There was another long silence. Alfonso half worried he'd pushed his point too far, but then he saw in Jennifer's eyes the acknowledgment that he was right on this one.

"OK, I admit, ... I admit that sometimes Petr could be sort of calloused about some of the more difficult people in church. But that lady really *is* difficult. I'm sure you've got those people in your church too." Jen gave him a penetrating glare, with "don't judge us" written all over face. Alfonso smiled and laughed, as if to say "of course!"

Jen went on, "But, how does this thing about saying 'the old bag' relate to feeling distant from God, and what does it have to do with finding Petr?" Jen asked, trying to quell the emotions by sounding business-like again.

"Don't you see Jen?" Alfonso began, hoping he didn't sound irritable (he really had to get some decent coffee soon). "To Petr, at least recently, both God and people have become *things*. He wasn't relating to them as persons. I mean, maybe he used to, but at least lately, he's treated both as things. He's been *using* God to fulfill his own agenda, and when God doesn't perform to his liking, he uses people, for a sense of significance. He used their approval, their satisfaction with him, to measure his well-being. He seems to either exploit people, like he did with the 'old bag,' or he ingratiates himself to people, like he's been doing with the board chair. This theme comes up again and again in his journal, Jen. And the two work in tandem: If God, the Creator, is just a distant thing to Him, then so are God's creations — things to be used."

Jen was starring wide-eyed now, straight at Alfonso, comprehension crashing over her. "I, I think maybe you're right, Al. As awful as it is to admit, I think you might actually be right about this."

"Now Jen, don't get me wrong here," Alfonso backpedalled slightly. "I know Petr loves you. He loves the kids; he loves me and he probably loves lots of other close people. But, the more I connect the dots, the more I see in Petr the pattern I've seen in other pastors who implode like this: these empty relationships with people and with God, in which people and God are just things to use.

"Jen, I realize I'm saying some harsh stuff, but here's the clue I'm seeing. Did you notice in this last entry I read, how Petr was plotting to go out in a way that will make others sorry; in a way that will stick in their imaginations?"

Jennifer winced at this, trying to ward off images of what this could mean.

Alfonso pushed on, "Jen, I think he's going to try to do something showy, something that won't be forgotten; something that'll stick in everyone's imagination."

He draw a deep breath and went on, "It's all part of using people like things, using their reaction to his suicide, in order to gain a sense of his own significance. It's part of using God like a thing, to do something connected with the church. Jen, I think he's going to try one last time to 'win over' the congregation and to use God to do it. I think he might try to kill himself at the church building."

The Self-in-Relation with the Creator and the Created

We argue that the third leg of biblical differentiation is the self's relationship with God and with others. This is more than adopting the correct beliefs about God. This is more than understanding God's view of our new identity in Christ. This means going a step further and nurturing one's connection with God and with others.

Countless Christian books have already been written over the centuries on the subject of nurturing our relationships with God and with others. Many of these books are better than this one. So, why we are dedicating a whole chapter to a well-trod subject?

In many ways, this third leg is the lynch pin of our whole model of biblical differentiation, so we do need a full chapter to demonstrate our particular viewpoint. From just a biblical standpoint alone, it could be argued that relationships are the heart of the entire Christian experience, especially given the way in which Jesus summarized our whole duty as simply to love God and love others (Matt. 22:37-39). Thus, your relationships with God and with others are never really a tired old subject. If your relationships are already perfect, then you probably don't need to read this chapter. But if you're like most of us and you've got room to improve your relationships, this chapter will be helpful.

From the point of view of understanding differentiation and its impact on your resiliency, life is all about relationships. In fact, life is *only* about relationships one could argue. Relationships are the only context in which differentiation can get worked out, nurtured and matured. By definition, differentiation is all about relationships because it is about learning to identity yourself as appropriately *different* than others. So, if you want to gain resiliency (the carrot we're dangling before you to keep you reading this book), then you need to know that you can only get more differentiated (and therefore more resilient), *in relationships.*

Non-Differentiated Relationships

You can understand why differentiation only happens in relationships when you take a closer look at the non-differentiated self. The non-differentiated self is a person who too closely identifies with another person or circumstance—someone who has become "fused" with another.

So, a man who identifies too closely with his wife won't have the inner strength to be resilient if his wife suffers and dies from cancer. This non-differentiated husband is dragged down into her suffering and suffers deeply himself because his soul is fused with hers. He cannot tolerate her suffering, and therefore suffers to a degree similar to her suffering. If she dies from the cancer, her death is no relief to the husband's suffering, at least not at first, because something essential in him dies with her.

"Wait a second," you might be thinking, "Isn't it a good thing to suffer with those who suffer? Aren't you just describing empathy? Isn't that what Jesus does with us—He empathizes with our suffering?"

Fusion and empathy are actually quite different things, as we'll make clear later in the chapter. True empathy is certainly a marker of healthy, differentiated relationships. And whenever a close, beloved partner dies, of course the survivor feels it and is devastated by it on the deepest level possible.

But in this scenario of a dying spouse, the difference between fusion and empathy is that the surviving fused person will feel more lost, disoriented, and crushed for much longer and to a far more severe degree than in a healthy, differentiated relationship. This sense of being crushed may actually reach the point in which a person feels unable to move on, recover and resume normal life.

You could argue that a life is never "normal" for any survivor, and you would be correct. But in a differentiated relationship, no matter how horrible the death or how close the relationship, the survivor is able to move on *eventually*. Life will be forever different for the survivor, but at least he or she can have hope of a new normal at some point in the future. It can never be the old normal, but nevertheless hope exists for a new kind of positive future.

The inability to move on lasts for a much longer time for those in fused relationships. Sometimes they never move on. Their capacity for living productive and fulfilling lives can be permanently diminished. In these cases, the impact on resiliency is obvious.

Even negative relationships, the kind we'd like to escape, are affected by fusion, to the detriment of our resiliency. Let us say a woman over-identifies with, or is fused with, an abusive husband. This means that she identifies too closely with his welfare and happiness. In other words, she has interwoven her own welfare and happiness so tightly with his that if he is unhappy she feels unhappy. It means she doesn't have the ability to feel happy or content with life apart from his feeling happy and content. This dynamic always appears illogical to those outside the relationship. But for those inside the relationship it makes sense.

No wonder it can be very difficult to leave an abuser. If she does depart for any length of time, she may find herself obsessing about who will do his laundry, cook his food and soothe his anger. Her own need to feel a measure of happiness, however small, is so closely intertwined with his that she can feel as if she's living in someone else's body when she's apart from her routine with him. She may see herself as the one human being capable of making him happy, and therefore necessary to his survival.

What's happening is that she sees her own survival inextricably linked to his. Against all reason, she may look to his approval as the affirmation she needs to feel good about her own existence. This is one of the shocking reasons for the famously common but inexplicable "battered-wife syndrome," in which an abused partner remains with an abuser. This is an extreme example of fusion. You can just imagine how this kind of fusion impacts an abused person's prospects for resiliency.

But fusion, or non-differentiation, occurs in much more subtle ways than outright abuse. It can be seen in the man who cannot be at peace with himself if there is any hint that his wife is unhappy with him. You'll often see this in younger couples that appear to love each other so deeply. They will say things like, "We're in such unity that I don't know where the other partner ends and I begin."

It can be seen in the parent who cannot release her children into adulthood when they go off to college. It can be seen in the child who is devastated by a single look of disapproval from a parent. It can be seen in the perfection-istic student who is crushed by an A minus because he's built his self-respect upon pleasing his teachers, and the "minus" is a clear sign of their disapproval.

It can be seen in the girl who cannot live happily without a boyfriend for more than a few days. It can be seen in the person who cannot enjoy a free Friday night if there is any hint that her friends are having fun without her. It can be seen in the pastor, like Petr, who cannot motivate himself to move forward when his church board disagrees with him.

People can also fuse with circumstances. We can feel our happiness and sense of self bound up inextricably with certain outcomes. We tend to fuse our significance with a desirable way in which we'd like to see situations turn out. A light-hearted example of this is the person who is inconsolable for days at the defeat of his favorite sports team. A more serious example might be the person who is unable to bounce back emotionally and move on from the failure of a business she started. There is the famous story of hundreds of stockbrokers who leaped to their deaths from their Wall Street offices on October 28, 1929, the day the US stock market dramatically crashed and ignited the Great Depression. These stockbrokers were so fused with the stock market prices that they lost the will to live when their financial losses became apparent.

All of this highlights the danger to resiliency posed by over-identifying, or being fused, with people and circumstances. Fused people feel more stress, anxiety and angst than differentiated people. This is because they over-identify with other things and people. They've entrusting their own sense of happiness and personal welfare too completely to others and to having circumstances play out in a certain way. This higher level of stress, anxiety, and angst makes it less likely that a person will recover triumphantly from trials. As long as someone's sense of happiness and well-being is tied up or fused with another person or circumstance, that someone's hope for resiliency is out of his or her own control.

This was a major part of why Petr found himself so trapped in his depression, and why suicide seemed like the best alternative to his misery. Petr's sense of his own well-being was fused with the approval of those in his church. This manifested itself in several ways. In his relationship with the board chair, Petr became ingratiating and deferential, even spineless in an effort to appease this man. In his relationship with many other congregants, Petr sought to achieve superstar status.

Petr's leadership behavior revolved around making people laugh and winning their favor. He became secretly contemptuous of those he couldn't charm into becoming his fans.

Both of these kinds of relationships demonstrate a non-differentiated self: Petr over-identified with his congregants, looking to them to provide his sense of significance through their approval. Without their approval, Petr felt "hollow" and without a sense of significance.

As Alfonso and Jennifer figured out, this fusion with congregants ultimately resulted in an attitude of disdain for them, in which they became mere things to be used. They were valuable to Petr insofar as they could provide his sense of significance. No wonder he felt "empty" when his relationships were such hollow shells. Other people were good only for his selfish exploitation.

You might object at this point by saying that we all have plenty of relationships that have been reduced down to a kind of mutual exploitation. We don't expect our relationship with our grocery store clerk to be filled with mutual respect and honor – we hand over money at the store and expect certain goods and services in return. This relationship, and many others like it, can be that simple and we don't feel the slightest bit violated for such agreed upon mutual exploitation.

But this chapter is talking about relationships that are supposed to mean more. We're talking about relationships with friends and family, with spouses, with fellow-believers who have all come together in the Name of Christ to live into His vision for His new community.

Sadly, over-identification with others leads inevitably to this kind of mutual exploitation. The person who is fused with his wife is in fact exploiting her for a sense of significance that he cannot, for whatever reasons, muster on his own. The person who is fused with her boyfriend is also exploiting him for that same sense of significance. Even if that boyfriend appears to be the one doing the exploiting, in actual fact both parties are mutually exploiting one another. This is because, just like the boyfriend, she stays in the relationship to get something very selfish from it. This selfish goal might be a sense of security, a sense that she's worthwhile to somebody, a way to protest her father's failure to love her, or a desire to backfill a black hole of emptiness in her heart. She thinks she is getting something out of the relationship, but in reality, this is a something that bears no resemblance to Jesus' command to love another.

This is the main difference between fusion and empathy. At its heart, fusion results in exploitation, however subtle and hard to detect. At its heart, empathy feels the pain of others for purely altruistic motives, for the sake of the other. The goal of empathy is to benefit the other. The goal of fusion is to benefit oneself. Truly empathic people do not depend on the other person to fill their needs and sense of personal emptiness.

"As I Have Loved You"

We contend that God has a different plan for relationships. It is a plan that does not center on mutual exploitation. It is not based on over-identifying with another. We contend that the more differentiated we are from one another, the more we are able to love one another truly. It is the ability to love one another to the same degree and fullness as Jesus commanded ("*as I have loved you*" – John 13:34, 15:12).

It is common to hear the objection: "Won't being differentiated ruin our ability to be intimate? Won't it make me feel detached and uncaring towards people?" But in reality, differentiation will enable us to love truly.

Generally speaking, even the best relationships can stand to grow in differentiation so they can look more like Jesus' model of relationship. Jesus loved in a selfless, non-biased, others-centered way. That is how He wants us to love.

It is common to claim that a particular relationship is purely a loving relationship, in imitation of Jesus. But the reality is that what appears to be love can be a bit of a masquerade. For instance, think of one stereotypical relationship dynamic: a grown man who hasn't been able to sever the apron strings from his mother.

Even in his adulthood, he acquiesces to the demands of the overbearing mother. He kowtows to her, even when he acknowledges that she makes him miserable. The fused mother and grown child appear to be held together *in the name* of loving one another. But what's really happening is that she, out of desperate insecurity and fear for her safety or fear of loneliness, uses every tool in her toolbox to manipulate and control her offspring to serve her. Her child is easily manipulated by guilt and shame and by his inability to imagine committed love coming from any other person. He is also motivated by insecurity and the fear of loneliness. He is probably motivated out of ignorance of what a healthy relationship could be like. Is this the love Jesus commanded of us?

Or think of the couple that seems infatuated with each other, that claims "We love each other so much that I can't tell where I end and other begins." While this kind of intimacy is certainly more pleasurable than in the previous example, at least at first, it has some built-in problems that end up suffocating both partners rather than setting each person free to thrive in the created and re-created selves.

Think of their apparently "intimate" relationship like two people trying to share the same sleeping bag. Have you ever tried to do that with someone? Were you able to have a full night of restful sleep that way?

Eventually one partner or the other realizes that there is only so much oxygen in that tight, enclosed space, and one of them needs to go up for air. But this need for air of course disturbs the delicately maintained harmony. As long as no one moves in the sleeping bag, everything is fine. There is peace. But as soon as someone moves to get air, the peace is broken. Understandably, the person who didn't feel the need for air pushes back or resists, and goodbye to a peaceful, harmonious night.

The point of this illustration is that the couple's "intimacy" is based on both parties suppressing their own created and re-created selves in favor of relational harmony. To keep this intoxicating sense of "peace," both partners must lay completely still and suppress the need for fresh air or movement. But that can't be maintained for long without considerable cost to one or both partners.

Then the harmony really gets disrupted when the partner who is still in the sleeping bag reacts negatively to the first partner moving up for air. The other's pursuit of simple breath is perceived as a threat to the peace.

In the same way, when one partner disturbs the apparently peaceful intimacy of a fused relationship, it is perceived as a life-or-death threat by the other. If the one going for air does somehow manage to reconnect with the created and re-created self, the partner still in the bag is in danger of losing that exquisite harmony that has been so important to existence.

So it comes as no surprise that the one still the bag responds "claws out," with the desperation of someone fighting for life, even if the partner searching for air becomes the target of those grasping claws. In short, the relationship implodes because the one unwilling to move toward health refuses to let the first one go.

Is this apparent "intimacy" anything close to imitating Jesus' standard of love?

Does fusion impact any of your relationships, limiting your capacity to keep Jesus' command to love others as He loved us?

Can you think of a time when your fusion with another limited your capacity for resilience? Has there ever been a time when fear of another's negative opinion or disapproval has kept you from telling her the full truth in love, even when this truth is what she most needs to hear? Has there ever been a time when you were so eager to gain another's positive opinion and approval that you did and said things you would not have otherwise, shrinking your integrity and thus making your love for the other less than selfless?

Or, have you ever felt threatened by another so that you avoid him, even when God is calling you to make a connection with him for the sake of the Kingdom? Are any of your close relationships tied together mostly by mutual exploitation — by an unspoken agreement that "you scratch my back and I will scratch yours"?

Do you want your relationships to more closely resemble what Jesus envisioned for us? Do you want them to be resilient?

The Secret to Differentiated Relationships

We believe that the secret to relationships that are differentiated, that are not based on mutual exploitation, is a relationship with God that does not treat God as an object to exploit.

If the relationship with God is right, then other relationships have the potential to be right. All good human relationships flow directly from a good relationship with God. Apart from a right relationship with God, our capacity for right relationships with others is reduced. The capacity for good human relationships is proportional to a good relationship with God.

"My relationship with God is right," you might confidently assert at this point. "I've received Jesus Christ as my Savior and I've bowed my knee to Him as my Lord. I have believed in Him and therefore have been given the right to be a child of God" (John 1:12). You would be entirely correct to assert this if you've authentically believed in Jesus. But we're not talking here about being positionally right with God. We're not talking about your regeneration or your salvation or your justification. We're talking about how you *relate* with, or *interact* with God. We're talking about cultivating a non-exploitative relationship with God.

Can people be in an exploitative relationship with God? Certainly. Don't many people base their faith in Him on how happy and satisfied He can make them feel? We trust Him when all is going well, but we can't find a way to trust Him when things go badly. In this case, God's value to us is reduced down to being a simple provider of happiness and contentment. He is not valued for His own sake, nor is His agenda a concern for us. He becomes an exploited thing.

But as Christian leaders, we've matured beyond that, haven't we? Have you ever used God, and your faith in Him, to publically justify your leadership initiatives? In other words, in order to sell a new idea or direction to your congregation, have you used God's name, and your position as His representative, as the ultimate endorsement to silence all opposition? This can be a form of exploitation.

King Saul famously did this in 1 Samuel 13, in order to quell the fears of his troops, who were beginning to scatter because there was no show of spiritual leadership. They were waiting for the prophet Samuel to appear and make a burnt offering and fellowship offerings. Saul saw the offerings as a way to soothe the people, as a way to convince them that God's favor was really with them in this hard pressed fight against the Philistines. But in verse 8 it says that Samuel was late. He had told Saul that he would be there in seven days, and he wasn't. So, King Saul went ahead and made the sacrifices himself, something that was forbidden for anyone who did not have a Levitical heritage.

Samuel was incensed and he gave Saul his first of many harsh rebukes. He even prophesied that Saul's kingdom would not be established nor would it endure and that another would be chosen as king (vs. 14) because of this violation.

But from a leadership perspective, we might think Saul's actions were warranted. Strategically speaking it was a good leadership move. The Israelite army was "quaking with fear" and had begun "to scatter" (vs. 7-8). They had clearly lost confidence that God was with them and would give them victory. Any good leader would try something like this to boost his followers' confidence psychologically. After all it wasn't as if Saul turned to false idols, like later kings did, to strengthen the hearts of his soldiers.

But it was exploitation of God never-theless. In this situation, God was reduced down to a *thing*: a provider of confidence. Saul's willingness to violate the Mosaic Law for the sake of keeping the army together was a sign that God's agenda mattered little to him. What did matter to him that day was victory against the Philistines. What did matter to him was his army's approval of his leadership. He needed his army to be confident so it could achieve the goal of victory.

Do any of our leadership moves ever resemble this mindset? Do we ever make decisions that seem strategically sound, that are calculated to achieve success, but which fail to take into account the actual will of the One we claim to serve?

A big reason for Petr's exploitative, fused treatment of people in his congregation was his exploitative treatment of God. However sincere and genuine his relationship with God had been earlier in his life, God had slowly become a thing that served Petr's own ambition and his need to feel successful and accepted.

Alfonso was wise to make this connection between Petr's attitude toward God and his attitude toward people. Insofar as we see God as a thing to be exploited, we will see people as things to be exploited. We will exploit others to the same degree that we exploit God. This attitude will drain our capacity for differentiated, non-fused relationships with others.

But we contend that the more your relationship with God can be authentic and non-exploitative, the more you will have an inner capacity to treasure humans for their own sake, in imitation of Jesus' example and in response to His command. We will explore how you can make your relationship with God (and with others) more authentic, in Chapter 9.

Summary

Thus far, we have laid out our three-legged stool of the biblically differentiated self. Each leg of the stool is necessary to support a fully differentiation that can be resilient in trials.

First, a highly differentiated person has more fully embraced her *created self*, that unique collection of strengths and weakness, preferences and dislikes, assets and liabilities that express who she really is. Embracing her created self means celebrating and appreciating her strengths. It also means responsibly accounting for her liabilities.

Second, a differentiated person has also more fully embraced his *re-created self*, the truths about one's new identity in Christ. Embracing it means that these biblical truths become more relevant than any other messages about his identity in shaping his perspective on and response to God, to life, and to self-understanding.

And finally, a highly differentiated person embraces her *self-in-relation* with God and with others. Embracing it means pursuing authentic, non-fused, non-exploitative relationships with God and others so she can be freed up to love God with *all* her heart, mind, soul and strength, and love others *as* Jesus loved her.

Chapter Five:
Jesus, the Differentiated and Differentiating One

Alfonso, Petr and Jennifer

Jennifer and Alfonso hardly talked as they drove through the streets toward the church. Both were lost in thought about the situation. Finally, Jennifer broke the silence: "Al, I'm not sure how this trip to the church will help us. I mean, Petr wouldn't try to do it today, with his birthday still a couple of days away. I mean, we're not going to find him hiding there. And the more I think about it, wouldn't our presence just raise suspicion?"

"Hmm. I suppose your right Jen," Alfonso replied. "Maybe we rushed here too quickly. But I'm sure we're going to find some clues at the church, so we'd end up going anyways. I am worried about the whole 'raising suspicions' thing though. Do you think we can come up with an excuse for being here?"

"I'll try to think of a clever ruse," she said in a deadpan, as if to say that her cleverness was the last possible miracle that her brain could perform right now.

"You'd better think fast. We're almost there—Oh! There's a coffee shop! We've got to stop and get some! Do they have good coffee?"

"Coffee? At this time in the afternoon? Aren't you in your mid-forties Al?"

"Age makes no difference when you're in love, Jen," Alfonso chuckled.

"Hmmm, speaking of idolatry... And besides, you drank almost a pot and a half of my coffee earlier today. Wasn't that enough?"

Alfonso diplomatically chose to avoid the question about the quality of her coffee and instead repeated, "Do they have good coffee?"

"It's OK, I guess. I don't go to that one often."

Al also diplomatically chose not to verbalize his current thought that Jen probably wouldn't even know good coffee if she tried some, and instead pulled into the drive-through line. After getting the largest cup they sold, they were back on their way. Alfonso began to feel a little sense of normalcy return with the first couple of sips. "Ah, now that's good coffee."

"You say that as if mine wasn't any good!" Jennifer said, sounding offended.

Alfonso's eyes went wide with the "I'm caught" look. He started to stammer something when Jennifer's phone startled them both. "It's my sister," She said with a worried tone in her voice. "The kids are probably calling on her phone to check in. They weren't expecting to spend the night with their cousins. I, I don't know what to say to them, Al. They're probably going to ask questions and wonder why Dad's not picking up his phone. But if I don't answer they're going to freak out about not talking to me. Ugh! Al, Petr better not kill himself, because there is no way I'd be able to handle being a single parent. Ever."

"One worry at a time Jen. Can't you just be vague with them?"

"I, I'll try. You obviously don't know my kids well … Hello? Hi honey! Having fun with your cousins?… Uh-huh … Well, I'm sure she'll share if you ask nicely honey. Remember, sweetie, that's a new toy for her. She just got it for her birthday, so of course she's going to be a little possessive at first … Uh-huh … Uh-huh … Well, maybe your older cousin will want to play that favorite game of yours … Uh-huh. I know you were surprised about staying with them honey, but it will only be for a night or two … I'm not sure how long sweetie … OK, let me talk to your brother and sister, and then I need to talk with Auntie Heather …"

By the time they'd arrived at the church where Petr served as senior pastor, Jennifer had wrapped up her phone conversation. She burst into fresh tears when she hung up.

"Al, I am so worried about their little hearts. This would break them. I mean, little Sofia, without her Daddy?!" More tears poured out, "And Johnny? I know he'd try to act all brave, but Al, this is the kind of stuff that just crushes kids. I cannot believe that Petr would walk out on them like this. If he doesn't kill himself, I am going to kill him!"

"I, I don't mean that" she quickly stammered "… I mean, I'm so mad at him for abandoning them. I mean, right now I *feel* like I could kill him myself if I could just get to him first … I mean, I don't know what I mean …"

Al put his hand on her shoulder and handed her the box of tissues. "It's going to be OK, Jen," he murmured quietly. They were silent for a while and then Alfonso asked, "Ready to go Jen?"

She nodded and sighed deeply and started to open the car door, but then caught herself in the car's rearview mirror. "Agh! I look horrible! They are totally going to know I've been crying. Yuck! What am I going to do?" Jennifer began wiping away running mascara, but Al couldn't help thinking her efforts were in vain.

"Isn't there a back entry to this place?" Alfonso said, handing her more tissues. Some kind of side door? There's gotta be, this place is so huge."

"Yes, but I don't know if it's already locked up or not. We're here kind of late. I only have a key for the main door."

"Let's check anyways," suggested Alfonso.

A side door proved to be open, so they slipped in quietly and made their way to Petr's office without running into anybody. "I always forget how huge this place is," Alfonso said when they got to the office and closed the door behind them. "I would *love* to have an office this big. It would sure make pastoral counseling easier. And a little conference table like this? That would be perf…"

143

"Al," Jen said abruptly, more business-like and calmer now. "What are we looking for here? Now that we're here, I don't even know what we're trying to accomplish." Her calm tone was an attempt to counteract a growing sense of panic rising up inside her. Being in Petr's office just reminded her of the hopelessness of the task, and she started to fret that someone on the church staff might discover what was going on. Their presence was just going to make it that much harder to keep things hidden, especially if they saw she'd been crying.

Al paused and said, "I'm not sure. Let's start by seeing what we can find on his computer. Maybe his browser history can tell us something?" Jennifer got busy with that as Alfonso glanced up at Petr's bookshelves. It was a pretty nice collection of books, but one book in particular caught his eye. "Oh, hey, I just read this book a couple of months ago! Petr must have taken my recommendation to heart and ordered it."

Jennifer rolled her eyes. She knew how easily Alfonso could get lost in a book. "Al," her tone took on that of a reprimanding schoolteacher, "we don't have time to waste on books. You're going to have to suppress your inner theology geek a little longer until we find Petr."

"Well-deserved indictment, madam barrister, but actually, I was thinking that this book might be another clue."

"Ugh! Al, seriously, none of your 'clues' have gotten us anywhere. I feel like we've wasted almost an entire day trying to unravel Petr's inner psychology, and we're no closer to him now than we were when you arrived!"

"Easy sister." Al tried to calm her. "My clues led us here, didn't they?"

"And 'here' is really stressing me out! I am so worried that at any moment someone is going to walk in here and see that I've been crying and they're going to start asking questions, and I am just going to start blabbing and give it all away, and..." Jennifer's voice had been getting higher and stronger as she went on, despite her effort to clamp down on it with a stage whisper. Finally, she paused and let out a long, slow sigh, "I'm sorry.... I, I am just so upset."

"Naturally, Jen. I would expect anyone in your situation to be screaming their head off right now," Al empathized.

"So, what is this clue from this book?" Jen asked, back to her business-like voice.

"Well, the book is about Jesus and differentiation."

"English, kind sir. English."

"Sorry. Differentiation is this psychobabble term. It means having relationships with people in which they can't control or manipulate you. It means relationship in which others cannot determine your happiness. It means being happy with yourself, content with yourself, as God made you, whether or not others approve of you or like you. It means having this solid sense of the real you, and therefore having the capacity to do what God's called you to do, even if others oppose you.

"I just read this book a few months ago and strongly suggested to Petr that he read it. It helped me make so much sense of so many aspects of pastoral ministry. It helped me make sense of my own self, as a pastor and, well, just as a person. I thought Petr might find it helpful in the middle of the depression he's been going through. Looks like it isn't even opened though. The plastic is still on it."

"Sounds like a confusing idea. Just the sound of the word makes me feel tired. And just how are Petr's whereabouts related to this diff, differentials? Differ..."

"Differentiation," Alfonso filled in for Jennifer. "I learned about it when I was going through therapy last year, and..."

"What?!" Jen interrupted. "YOU went through therapy? Al, I thought you had a really strong faith? I'm shocked."

"Oh, Jen, please. This is not 1980 anymore, when therapy for Christians was thought to be as pagan as the Church of Satan. I started because I realized that if I could recommend counseling for some of my own parishioners whose problems were too big for me, then I should be willing to go through it myself. And I was struggling through several issues anyways. I needed another pair of eyes on them so I decided to give it a try. And I got a ton out of it. I told Petr all about it."

"Oh? And what did he say."

"He reacted just like you did."

"No surprise there. I did try to get him to go to marriage counseling once, years ago. He freaked and said it would be a bad example for the leader of the church to show his weakness by going to marriage counseling. He kept saying 'we can work this out ourselves honey.' You would have thought I'd asked him to try on a pair of thumb screws."

"I remember that." Al said ruefully.

"Well," Jen sighed, bringing herself back to the task at hand, "I guess this isn't the most shocking revelation of the day. And how is it a clue again?"

"The reason this book is a clue is that it's about how Jesus was the most differentiated person of all. He was the ultimate example of a differentiated person. It says that a big part of imitating or following Him is to work on our own differentiation."

"I still don't get how something that reminds me of 'differential equations,' my least favorite subject in college, can be a good thing."

"Oh, it's good all right Jen. And best of all, Jesus is not only the model of differentiation: He's the means of it!"

"Huh? You're getting more confusing instead of less. And it's still not clear to me how it is a clue Al."

"Well, just let me see if I can explain, Jen," Al began. "I just preached on this, so it's all fresh in my mind."

"*You* preached about psychobabble, Al? Now that *really* surprises me."

Alfonso laughed. "I only preach on something insofar as I think it's biblical, Jen. And this book here thoroughly convinced me that it *is* biblical. That, combined with the fact that working on my own differentiation helped me with so many things, pushed me to preach on it. I'm convinced it's the next horizon of spiritual growth for my congregation."

"Hmm. I guess that is kind of interesting Al. OK, so explain."

"Remember how Jesus was able to stand up to the Pharisees, the people who controlled Jewish public opinion in those days? Or, remember Jesus' ability to confront the crowds?"

"Sure, like when He called the Pharisees 'white-washed tombs' to their faces in Matthew 23? Or when Jesus called the crowd a 'brood of vipers' in John 8?"

"Exactly. You see, Jesus' ability to confront His opposition, to stand up for what is right and true, despite public opinion, despite their contempt and the worry over His safety, is a sign of Jesus' differentiation. And remember how Jesus had to stand up to His own family a few times?"

"Sure, like when He was kind of sassy to his own parents in Luke 2. Or like when He basically told off His family in Mark 3?"

"You're good with the Scripture addresses, Jen."

"Hey, it pays off, all those years of going through Awana as a kid, and then basically running the Awana ministry here for a decade." Jen said, smiling at the first really positive memory of the day.

"So, the point of this book is that Jesus was able to do all that confronting because He was so well differentiated. A differentiated person can tell others hard truths and stick to his guns and confront power or be brave in many dangerous situations because he doesn't see those things as real threats to his personhood, to his identity.

"Remember in John 19" he continued, "when Pontus Pilate was amazed at Jesus' lack of fear of him, so he told Jesus 'Don't you realize I have the power either to free you or to crucify you?' and Jesus responded by saying 'You would have no power over me if it were not given to you from above.' That was Jesus unafraid of what a powerful person could do to Him because He was confident that His real fate lay in the hands of His Father. He knew that another's threats didn't have real power over Him, because, like He'd said earlier in John 10 'I lay down my life. ... No one takes it from me, but I lay it down of my own accord. I have authority to lay it down and authority to take it up again.'"

Jennifer nodded, looking thoughtful now as she reflected on Alfonso's words.

"Jesus could confront because He was free from the fear of human opinion. He saw His future and His welfare as *different than* what people thought of him or *different than* what they could do to Him. That's where the word 'differentiation' comes from, by the way. All this made Him fearless in the face of human threats."

"Sounds freeing," Jen muttered wistfully.

"Believe me, it is, Jen." Alfonso went on, "But Jesus' differentiation also led to His ability to do the opposite thing — to comfort. Remember how He physically touched lepers?"

"Yeah," Jen jumped in. "Like in Mark 1:40-45, and in Luke 5:12-14? Their disease made them social outcasts, and so it was crazy for a person to touch them physically, because that would make Him a social outcast too."

"Correct!" Alfonso continued, "And remember how the woman with the issue of blood in Mark 5 was also a social outcast, and so it was terribly scandalous for her to touch Jesus? Or remember the woman with the immoral lifestyle in Luke 7 and how Jesus offended the Pharisees by letting her wipe His feet with her hair?"

"Yes! I love that story!"

"Well, Jesus could get close to people, even to the undesirable people who could have ruined His reputation for holiness. He could even get close to those who could have endangered Him with their diseases. This was because He was so well differentiated. Differentiation helps us do two opposite things. It helps us stick to our guns and bravely confront the darkness in other people, because that darkness is no real threat to us. *And* it helps us comfort others, drawing close to them in intimacy, because again, closeness is no longer a threat to us. Jesus could do both."

"Hmm. I'm sort of starting to see what you're talking about Al. You're talking about seeing people so that neither their darkness or their closeness is a threat. That sounds like that could be really freeing. But what exactly is differentiation again?"

"It is this inner, emotional state of being free from others' opinions, and therefore free from their control. It's when you don't care about their approval *or* their disapproval. It doesn't matter if others like or dislike you, because your sense of self doesn't come from or rely on what they think of you. You can be confident in yourself with or without their favor."

"Humph—sounds freeing, but also kind of secular Al, no offense."

"None taken. That's how lots of people in my congregation have been reacting since I started this sermon series. I'm not surprised."

"Yikes! Doesn't that worry you Al? Your congregation giving you negative feedback about your sermons? I mean, that would just kill Petr. He absolutely can't stand it when someone tries to pick a fight with him over a sermon. It just sends him down this spiral of despair."

"That is exactly my point, Jen. I think Petr reacts that way because he is not differentiated from his parishioner's opinions and approval. In other words, he doesn't see his own self-worth, his own sense of who he is, as *different than* their like or dislike of him.

Jen stared at him, so we went on, "I mean, he doesn't feel like his selfhood is *different than* the approval of others."

"Yeah, yeah, I get where the word 'different-ious' (or whatever) comes from now, thank very much for the lesson."

"It's *'differentiation'* Jen."

"Whatever. And I suppose you're above it all, Al? You don't ever struggle with what others think about you? It just doesn't affect you like it does the rest of us mere mortals? You just imitate Jesus so perfectly that you're never bothered by others?" The tone of annoyance was beginning to return to her voice as she was growing defensive of her husband again.

"No, Jen, of course I care about what others think. Of course it bothers me when they dislike me. But through therapy, and with this book, and of course by the grace of God through Jesus and the Spirit, I've really been able to grow in differentiation. Of course I'm not as good at it as Jesus was, and of course I never will be. But I feel like I am making some real progress in it.

"You know Jen," he continued, "it all began during a season when I was just feeling so spiritually dry, and I was really seeking after God. I felt like I didn't have the inner capacity to do all He was calling me to do. I felt like I either needed to expand on the inside, so to speak, or I needed to find another job. I was crying out to God for wisdom, for guidance, for help. Out of that season, I actually felt led by God to this Christian therapist. I took it as part of His answer to my seeking His face. It was all part of this big season of spiritual renewal for me."

Jen was listening intently, but still with the skepticism on her face.

"I mean, Jen, criticism still stings of course. But I don't *depend on* what others think about me as much I used to. I'm a lot more able to leave their criticism at the office when I go home at night so that it won't haunt me and steal my sleep like it used to. I'm a lot more able to be confident and happy with what I'm doing for God. Also, my ability to lead the church is noticeably better than ever because now I feel like I have the capacity to rise above criticism and keep pursuing the right direction. It also helps me re-direct myself when the criticism is true, because I've got less invested in *appearing* like I'm in the right—do you know what I mean?

"Jen, I am in no way saying I'm better than anyone. And of course, Jen, I give all credit to God. This has all been God graciously working in me through His love. It feels like *He* initiated it, not me. It's all been about Him, from beginning to end."

"Sorry Al for being critical. It's just that, I guess if I'm honest, what you're saying sort of pin points a big flaw I see in me and in Petr. I guess it sort of hurts to have this flaw exposed."

"No worries, Jen. See, you're taking a step toward differentiation right now, by choosing to not be defensive."

"But Al, you're missing the very important point that Jesus was *divine*. So, how are we supposed to imitate His diff, differential--however-you-pronounce-it- thing when He was divine?"

"Ah, but Jesus was fully divine *and* fully human, Jen! That is what this book is mostly about. The whole doctrine of the Incarnation is the secret behind Jesus' ability to be differentiated. Remember how He was 100% faithful to His divine nature, never leaving it behind? He maintaining His connection to His Heavenly Father the whole time? Well, He was also able to fully enter our reality and become one of us entirely."

"Keep going…"

"Well, like Jesus, when we've been born from above, born again by His Spirit, with a new nature and a new heart, we have this divine nature…"

"Whoa! Hold it right their Al! You're starting to sound pretty New Age-y," Jen protested.

"Just listen! Of course I don't mean we're gods, like Jesus is God. I mean that we have His divine nature living in us, and we're new creations that now have His mind, His Spirit, His own heart in us. Come on, Jen, that's pretty standard evangelical orthodoxy right there."

"OK, OK, keep going." Jen was hungry for something Al was communicating, even if she didn't fully understand it yet.

"Well, our new, re-created self restores and re-energizes our old, created-self to its proper functioning, so that all our God-given gifts and talents, personality traits and other special qualities unique to us are now brought under the service of God."

"Right. I'm still following."

"And if we hold closely to this new center of ourselves, this center that God created and then re-created in Christ, then we can walk in the kind of freedom Jesus did, and like Him enter into the reality of others."

"So, are you saying that if we hold onto this divine, re-created center of ourselves, then we'll be able to 'incarnate' into the lives of others like Jesus did?"

"Yes! Jen that is exactly what I am saying! Like Jesus, we can be brave in the face of danger because we can secretly assure ourselves that our life is "hidden in Christ," like in Colossians 3, and that our true essence is untouchable. So, we have the ability to confront darkness in others like Jesus did, and we have the ability to comfort those in need like Jesus did. And we can do this in a sustainable way, because we no longer have to fear needy people sucking our life out of us."

Jen was nodding, imagining the possibilities of living this way. A glimmer of hope was starting to rise in her. Al went on, "And of course, Jen, living this way, truly living it, is impossible apart from Jesus Himself. You know, like everything else in the Christian life, He is both the model and means of differentiation."

"Yeah, you said that already Al. What did you mean by saying that He is the 'means'"?

"You know Jen, like when Jesus told His disciples 'I am the vine, you are the branches. You can do nothing apart from me' in John 15? We can only grow in differentiation when we stick close to Jesus and walk tightly with Him, trusting Him for everything and drawing on Him for everything. He has the power, the resources, the wisdom. Only He can cause us to grow in this ability to be both courageous and comforting."

They were quiet for a long time as Jen gazed out the office window. She wasn't sure yet why Alfonso's words made her hungry for something more, but this freedom that he described poked a little pinprick of hope in her. It was tiny, but real. As small as it was, she began to wonder if possibly, just maybe, there was a way out of her own unending nightmare.

Suddenly, the door opened and in came Janice, the short, plumb, greying office manager of the church.

"I thought I heard someone in here." Janice took one look at Jennifer and asked, "Why Jen, are you OK?"

"Oh, uh, um… allergies. Terrible. Worst I've ever had. Just terrible."

"Oh, sorry to hear that. I should ask my husband for you what he uses for that. Whatever it is, it's really helped him a lot. It has worked wonders, actually. But isn't the hay fever season mostly over by now?" She turned to Alfonso, "And I recognize you. Aren't you Pastor Wolansky's friend, Pastor Alonzo Hernandez?"

"It's Alfonso. Alfonso Sanchez. I get that a lot, actually. Ha ha, that's OK. Yes, Petr and I served together as missionaries in Africa back in the day, and we went to seminary together. It's been several years since I've seen you Janice — good to see you again. I'm just visiting Indianapolis from out of town. Thought I'd stop by and say hi to the family."

"Well, welcome to town Alonzo. Hope you enjoy your visit. Or, I guess I should say 'bienvienedos'?"

"Haha" Alfonso fake-laughed. "I get that a lot too. I was actually born right here in America. Right here in Indiana in fact. I hardly speak Spanish at all. I almost forgot it all even though my parents spoke it at home. English is definitely my first language."

"Of course, how nice," Janice said absentmindedly. "And I am so glad you came by Jen," Janice said turning back to her. "Petr told me this morning he thought you'd be by sometime today."

"What?" Jen asked, trying not to sound too shocked. "You … you saw Petr *today*?"

"Well, yes. He dropped by to get a few things before he took off. Said he had some important meetings all today and tomorrow. Said he wouldn't be reachable by cell phone. Kind of odd, you know. He is always available for church business by his cell phone. But he is such a busy man. I guess I don't need to tell *you* that Jen. I mean..."

"Janice," Jennifer broke in, "Did Petr say anything about where he was going?"

"No, he didn't. Which is kind of unusual. Normally, all his meetings are on my calendar. But none of these meetings are on it this time." Janice cleared her throat and then asked, hesitantly, "Jen, is everything OK?"

"Everything's just fine Janice," Jennifer said too quickly to be believable. "And, um, why exactly did Petr tell you he thought *I* would be by today?"

"Oh, yes, he said he thought you'd come by looking for him and that he had a note for you. I thought it was odd that he thought you'd be looking for him, but of course I didn't ask him any questions." Janice had a sterling reputation for discretion. "Just a minute, I'll go grab the note for you. It's in the main office."

The second she closed the door behind her, Jennifer and Alfonso turned to each other with wide eyes and wide mouths, both too stunned to say anything out loud for a moment. Finally, Jen mumbled, "Al, this is unbelievable. Petr was here this morning, and he somehow anticipated that I might show up here looking for him."

"OK, Jen, so, it's like we're on his trail. And Janice said something about him picking something up. Jen, when she comes back, be sure to ask her what it was he was picking up."

"What I don't understand it how he got here. He didn't take the car."

"I suppose he could've taken a taxi, or Uber or Lyft or something like that?" Al offered.

"But how'd he do that without his cell phone?"

"Maybe he's had a burner phone that you don't know about?" The two fell into silence.

A moment later Janice came back with the note. As Jennifer was taking it from her she asked, "Janice, what was it that my husband drove this morning?"

"Oh, I thought that was funny too. He came and left in one of those ride-sharing services. He said something about your car being in the shop. But of course you would've known about that. Jennifer, is everything OK?" This time Janice's tone of voice was more probing.

"Oh, I was just checking to see if the taxi thing worked out for him. You know, how unreliable those services can be. Yes, yes, our car is in the shop. It's a, a broken... a ...broken tire, I mean carburetor, thing-a-ma-jigger-thingy..."

There was a long, tense silence as Janice stared intently at Jen, and Jen tried hard not to meet her gaze.

Alfonso finally broke in, "Say, Janice, just wondering what Petr was picking up this morning? You see, it was actually something for me, for my ministry, to help me with my, ah, ministry, and he promised me that it was going to come today."

Jennifer began breathing normally again once Alfonso got them back on track.

"Oh, it was just something from a little unmarked box that arrived first thing this morning, special delivery. I don't know what it was. Pastor Wolansky has been very anxious for some time for that box to arrive. He kept asking me every day for the past week if it had come in. He called me this morning before coming in to inquire about it. When I said it had come, he said 'I'll be there soon. Don't open it, under any circumstances.' It took him a while to get here, I guess because of the taxi. But when he did, he opened it in private. I didn't see what was in it. I already broke down that box and put it in the recycling."

"Oh, of course he was anxious to receive it, because he knew I was coming this weekend. Whew. Sounds like it came just in time!" Alfonso's voice was full of mock cheer. "Ah, Janice," Alfonso asked, "Could we take a look at that box in recycling?"

"Well, sure. I guess. I don't see why not. Follow me."

"Jen, you read that note while I go look at the box." Alfonso left the room after Janice.

Jennifer reluctantly opened the note as the knot of dread seemed to tighten inside her stomach. She took a deep breath and began to read. The words seemed to swim on the page and she had to re-read it several times before she could register its meaning. When it finally became clear, Jennifer felt like a new wave of helplessness crashed over her. More tears came as she put her head in her arms on Petr's desk.

Three minutes later, Alfonso returned. Jennifer stood up, clutching the note tightly to herself. "Al, you're not going to believe this..." she began. But then she looked up and saw Alfonso. His eyes were wide and all the color had drained from his face. He was also holding a piece of paper — it looked like a packing slip — but all he could do was point at it silently. "A..., Al...?"

Alfonso pointed at the packing slip more emphatically, still silent. He obviously couldn't get a word out. At first, Jennifer couldn't figure out what he was saying, but then her eyes slid to the top, left hand corner, where she read: "Arcadia Machine and Tool AMT Hardballer Pistol, .50 Action Express."

Jesus, the Model and the Means

Jesus provides us with the ultimate model of a differentiated person. He is also the means to becoming more differentiated. Seeing Jesus at the center of this whole idea is critical if we are to cultivate our own biblical differentiation.

Jesus the Model

As Alfonso explained to Jennifer, Jesus demonstrated the fruit of differentiation in two main ways. He could bravely confront, free from the fear of reprisals, and he could bravely comfort, again free from the fears associated with intimacy. Jesus' incarnation was the secret to this ability.

Jesus could confront the darkness in other people. Alfonso and Jennifer already rehearsed several of the most prominent examples of this. These confrontations had dire consequences, since we know they led directly to His crucifixion. The different factions in Jerusalem finally conspired to put an end to His life after years of enduring the confrontations.

But as Alfonso pointed out about Jesus' encounter with Pontius Pilate, the very real threat these enemies posed to Jesus' welfare was not a threat to Jesus' very identity. Therefore, though He was aware that His opponents could take His physical life, He also knew that He and no one else was in charge of laying down His own life. Even though humans could and did destroy His body, Jesus was firmly confident that "No one takes it from me" (John 10:18).

Jesus had the perspective, expressed to Pilate, that "You would have no power over me if it were not given to you from above" (John 19:11). This confidence prevented Jesus from shrinking away from His duty to confront evil. This has been the secret strength of Christian martyrs ever since the First Century.

Jesus' ability to be intimate with and to comfort the most outcast, the most diseased, the most ostracized, also came from this same confidence in who He was and in His Father's sovereign control over events. Touching lepers presented a real danger of disease transfer, but worse than that was the potential for social ostracism in the First Century Jewish mind. Being touched by the woman with the hemorrhage also carried the danger of ostracism. Association with the woman who wiped His feet with her hair carried with it the real possibility that Jesus would lose His religious credibility, not just before the Pharisees but also before all Jews, since most of them had adopted the Pharisees' outlook on correct religious practice.

Jesus' insistence on doing many of these things on the Sabbath got Him into more hot water, earning Him the permanent scorn of the Pharisees and many others. But in spite of these threats, Jesus confidently touched those who needed the touch of heaven. He loved the unlovable and comforted those in need. And He did it whenever and wherever and to whomever the Father led Him, despite the rules the Pharisees' had added to the Mosaic Law about Sabbath keeping.

What was the secret behind Jesus' ability to both bravely confront and bravely comfort?

As Alfonso pointed out, Jesus' incarnation was the secret behind this ability. When Jesus became one of us, fully human in every way, He never gave up being fully God. His whole time on earth He remained one hundred percent faithful to His true, eternal self, the Second Person of the Trinity, God the Son, the living Word of God. But simultaneously He was able to step into our reality and fully take on human nature and all the troubles of humanity without any compromise. This is the mystery of the Incarnation.

In his letter to the Philippians, Paul describes how Jesus, beginning with His confidence and security in His relationship with the Father ("who, although He existed in the form of God"), was able to relinquish that exalted status because He was so secure in it: "did not regard equality with God something to be grasped." This allowed Him to, "empt[y] Himself, taking the form of a bond-servant ... He humbled Himself by becoming obedient to the point of death, even death on a cross" (Phil. 2:6-7). This self-humiliation on behalf of others flowed from Jesus' secure relationship with His Father.

While on earth, Jesus remained perfectly united with His Father's will at all times ("I and the Father are one," John 10:30. See also John 10:38, 14:11, and 14:20). Jesus was faithful to speak only God's explicit will ("The words I say to you I do not speak on my own initiative, but the Father abiding in Me does his works," John 14:10). Jesus was faithful to do only as the Father directed Him ("I do exactly as the Father commanded me," John 14:31).

From this, Jesus was able to lay down His life: "Even as the Father knows Me and I know the Father; and I lay down My life for the sheep" (John 10:15). Jesus' self-denial and sacrifice on behalf of others flowed from his secure intimacy with His Father. "Jesus, knowing that the Father had given all things into His hands, and that he had come forth from God and was going back to God, got up from supper, and laid aside His garments; and taking a towel, He girded Himself" (John 13:3-4). Jesus could serve in a manner reserved for the lowliest slave because he knew His purpose, origin and destiny.

In imitation of Jesus, Paul was able to give everything for the sake of the Gospel. Secure in his identity as an adopted and beloved child of God (see his logic in Eph. 1 and Rom. 8), Paul was able to lay aside his more superficial identity as a "Hebrew of Hebrews" (Phil. 3:5. See also 2 Cor. 11:22), and engage the Gentile culture where it was at, in all its idolatry (Acts 17:22-23). His security in Christ allowed him to be flexible, comfortable with the ambiguity of cross-cultural ministry, and willing to adjust himself for the sake of others (1 Cor. 9:22). Unlike Petr, Paul's ability to "become all things to all men" reflected an inward security in Christ, versus an insecure grasping after others' approval.

Jesus' faithfulness to His divine nature is analogous to our faithfulness to our created and re-created selves. His Incarnation is analogous to our self-in-relation with others. When we have the emotional maturity to enter into another's reality with true empathy, compassion and the kind of love Jesus demands of us (John 14:13), we are in some small measure experiencing what Jesus experienced when He entered our reality in His Incarnation.

The Incarnation is significant for many essential things in the Christian faith. But regarding our differentiation it is significant because it models the ability to be faithful to our created and re-created selves, as well as how to be in relationship with others. This is a level of emotional health that God always intended for His people to experience.

On the surface, entering into another's reality, or incarnating with another, sounds a bit like the fusion of what an undifferentiated person experiences. Undifferentiated people, because they are out of touch with their created and re-created selves, can easily disappear into another, more dominant person. Their anxiety and fear leaves them susceptible to getting swept up into another's stronger personality. This can look like incarnation.

But as we explained earlier, their apparent empathy is actually an insecurity that leads them to seek significance in another. The critical difference between such people and Jesus was that He could empathize with others without ever losing touch with His true self. In fact, He can empathize with the entire human race that has or ever will exist, to the point of fully taking on our reality and becoming one of us, without it detracting from His divinity for one instant. Despite His incarnation, He never lost touch with His purpose or true nature. He never stopped being God.

In contrast, the person with a low level of differentiation disappears into another's reality precisely because he is out of touch with his true self. In the absence of any substantial reality in his own heart, he must, like a parasite, live off the life force of another.

Like Jesus, a highly differentiated person can enter into the reality of another, can incarnate himself into another's struggles, pains and joys to the point of being a true help, precisely because he is firmly in touch with his created and re-created self. It is from this place of confidence that you can boldly venture forth into another's life, either to confront or to comfort, without danger of losing yourself.

Jesus the Means

As Alfonso explained carefully to Jennifer, Jesus is not only the model of differentiation. He is also the *means* to greater differentiation. As with everything in the Christian life, Jesus is "the way, the truth, and the life" (John 14:6). Biblical differentiation, like all true spiritual and emotional growth, can only happen through Jesus.

As part of Jesus' final instructions to His disciples before the crucifixion, in John 13-17, He clarified for them the means by which they were to be fruitful for Him. He had commanded them to bear fruit, fruit that "would remain" (John 15:16). It was to be fruit that proved the authenticity of their discipleship to Rabbi Jesus and it was to be fruit that glorified God the Father (vs. 8).

But Jesus did not leave them alone in this impossible task. He promised that He Himself would be their means of bearing this fruit that He demanded. Jesus promised to be the very supply of that which He required from them. He would be the source of the fruit He expected from them. By using a metaphor in which He called Himself a "vine" (vs. 1 and 5) and His disciples "branches" (vs. 4-5), Jesus created a simple and vivid picture: as a branch cannot bear fruit apart from its vine, neither could they bear fruit apart from Jesus. In this way He explained the direct dependency of the disciple on Jesus to live in a way that pleases Him.

In order to access Jesus as their source, Jesus commanded His disciples to "abide" in Him, as a branch abides in a vine (vs. 4). This word "abide" means to take up residence, or to settle down and dwell in a place permanently. In this context, it conjures up an image of a branch inseparably connected to its vine.

Jesus described this kind of connection with several other phrases. In the immediate context of this passage, He described abiding as His words living in the disciples' hearts (vs. 7), as the disciples clinging to His love, (vs. 9), and as them keeping His commandments (vs. 10), as any first century Jewish rabbi expected of his disciple.

Earlier in John, Jesus described abiding with another metaphor, that of eating and drinking Him (6:56). In this analogy (vs. 35-58), Jesus calls Himself the bread of heaven and that by eating and drinking Him a person might have eternal life. He declares at the beginning of this teaching "he who comes to me will not hunger, and he who believes in Me will never thirst" (vs. 35). In other words, we eat and drink Jesus when we come to Him and when we believe in Him.

Coming to Him and believing Him means looking to Him to be all He says He is. It means to depend on Him for sustenance with the same intensity with which we depend on physical food and drink for our basic welfare. It means to rely on Him to be our entire resource, our hope, our rock, our wisdom and power and sanctification (1 Cor. 1:24 and vs. 30). In summary, it means looking to Him to be our "all in all" (1 Cor. 15:28).

One of Paul's metaphors to describe how Jesus is the source of all is his picture of the church as the body of Christ (1 Cor. 12:12-27, Eph. 4:15-16). As a part of this metaphor, he depicts Christ as the body's "head," apart from which no life can occur in the rest of the body. Paul writes it this way:

Him who is the head, even Christ, from whom the whole body, being fitted and held together by what every joint supplies, according to the proper working of each individual part, causes the growth of the body for the building up of itself in love (Eph. 4:15-16).

In other words, Christ the head of the body is the ultimate source of its growth and health and vitality.

Several of the New Testament authors made this idea of Jesus as *the* source more explicit with their frequent use of phrases like "*through* Jesus." John used it in his Gospel, saying, "grace and truth came *through* Jesus Christ" (John 1:17). Luke explained "the good news of peace" came "*through* Jesus Christ" (Acts 10:36). Paul used it many times, like when he wrote the Romans that their peace with God came "*through* our Lord Jesus Christ" (Rom. 5:1). He told them it was "*through* Christ Jesus" that "the law of the Spirit who gives life has set you free from the law of sin and death" (Rom. 8:2). To the Corinthians he wrote that grace was

given them *"through* Christ Jesus"* (1 Cor. 1:4)
and that their "victory" came *"through* our Lord
Jesus Christ"* (1 Cor. 15:57). He told them that it
was *"through"* Jesus Christ that "all things came"
and that it was *"through"* Him that they lived (1
Cor. 8:6). In his second letter to them, Paul
wrote, "you *through* His poverty ... become rich"
(2 Cor. 8:9).

Paul wrote to the Ephesians, explaining
that their predestination to the son-ship of God
came *"through* Jesus Christ"* (Eph. 1:5). He told
the Philippians that they would be "filled with
the fruit of righteousness that comes *through*
Jesus Christ"* (Phil. 1:11). He told Titus that the
Holy Spirit and His saving, regenerating work is
"poured on us generously *through* Jesus Christ
our Savior"* (Tit. 3:6). The author of Hebrews
said that people are made "holy *through* the
sacrifice of the body of Jesus Christ once for all"
(Heb. 10:10). Later the same author wrote that
God "equips you with everything good for
doing his will, and ... [He] work[s] in us what is
pleasing to him, *through* Jesus Christ"* (Heb.
13:21). Peter explained that our new birth into
the living hope happens *"through* the
resurrection of Jesus Christ from the dead"* (1
Pet. 1:3). All these authors are saying that the
benefits and blessings of being a Christian,
including the capacity for fruit bearing, come
through Jesus. This is true of differentiation as
well. It comes *through* Jesus.

Many of the New Testament authors also seem delighted to use the phrase "*in* Jesus" to describe our dependence on Jesus to be the means of our spiritual advancement. This seems to have been one of Paul's favorite phrases. He told the Romans that they are "alive to God *in* Christ Jesus" (Rom. 6:11). Later he described how the very "love of God" was "*in* Christ Jesus our Lord" (Rom. 8:29). He explained to the Corinthians that their sanctification would come "*in* Christ Jesus" (1 Cor. 1:2).

Paul told the Ephesians that God accomplished His "eternal purpose ... *in* Christ Jesus our Lord" (Eph. 3:11). In his letter to the Philippians, when he famously tells them that God will meet all their needs, he explains that God will do so "according to the riches of his glory *in* Christ Jesus" (Phil. 4:19).

Peter wrote to his audience in his second letter that their effectiveness and productivity for God would happen "*in* their knowledge of our Lord Jesus Christ" (2 Pet. 1:8). Again, as with the "through" passages, the phrase "in Jesus" points to this idea that Jesus is the very means of spiritual progress.

Plenty of other New Testament writings in one way or another confirm this truth that God is the means of Christian fruitfulness. For instance, Paul told the Corinthians that it was God Himself who would "keep you firm to the end" (1 Cor. 1:8). Peter explained "if anyone serves, they should do so with the strength *God* provides" (1 Pet. 4:11). As with everything in the Christian life, there is no progress in any form of spiritual maturity, no growth in our fruit bearing capacity, no sanctification, apart of deep intimacy with Jesus.

Some people protest that it is hard to have intimacy with Jesus because He is no longer physically present on earth. Jesus has ascended, and therefore all we have are four interesting biographies of Him. But with His ascension, the Holy Spirit was identified as Jesus' agent of fruitfulness instead of God the Son. In John 14:16-18 and 16:7-15, Jesus talks about the Holy Spirit as coming to replace Him as the immediate presence of God on earth. Instead of Jesus being physically present on earth to reveal God to humanity, God the Spirit now mediates God's presence here. Jesus has promised to be with His people *through* His Holy Spirit. So it is by means of the closeness, the proximity, of God the Spirit that His work gets done in and through His people.

Paul makes this idea a central part of his theology. In Romans 5:5 he describes how we experience the love of God in our hearts *through* the mediation of the Holy Spirit. Later in this letter (14:17) he tells the Romans that we experience righteousness, peace and joy *in* the Holy Spirit. Paul also tells the Thessalonians that they experience joy during tribulation *in* the Holy Spirit (1 Thess. 1:6). He tells Titus that our experience of being washed "in regeneration and renewing" (3:5) has been done *by* the Holy Spirit. In summary, the work of Jesus to be our true vine and to produce His fruit in us is carried out through the Holy Spirit in us.

Paul describes this activity between Jesus and the Spirit as an indivisible partnership, in which we can't quite see where One ends and the other begins. Read through his description of the Spirit's actions in us in the first part of Romans 8, for instance. In verse 9 he talks about the Spirit dwelling in us. But in the very next verse, he says, "Christ is in you." Then he's back to the Spirit dwelling in us in the following verse. Which is it? Both. God the Son and God the Holy Spirit partner together to do God's work in His people. In Ephesians 2:18, Paul expresses this idea as having access to the Father "*through* Jesus" and "*in* one Spirit."

Perhaps biblical differentiation as we've laid it out so far seems intimidating to you. Perhaps it appears far off and unattainable. But as with any fruit, we make progress in differentiation and therefore resiliency "through Jesus" and "in the Spirit." God works this differentiation in us by means of His Spirit inside of us. Therefore, we encourage you to strengthen your connection with Jesus through simple faith. As He taught us, it only takes the tiniest mustard seed of faith (Matt. 17:20, Luke 17:6), properly placed, to draw closer to Him. And the good news is that He eagerly invites us all closer (Matt. 11:28-30; Heb. 4:16, 10:22; James 4:8).

We also encourage you to open your heart more fully to the power of the Holy Spirit in your life. In the story of Philip's evangelization of the region of Samaria (Acts 8:4-24), it says that the Apostles prayed for them to receive the Holy Spirit (vs. 15). This is strange, because it says that they had already "received the word of God" (vs. 14), and had "been baptized in the name of the Lord Jesus" (vs. 16). But the text shows that "He (the Spirit) had not yet fallen upon any of them" (vs. 16) prior to this point. A similar story is told in Acts 19:1-6.

Is it possible that our lack of power to be fruitful for God is due to having inadequately received the fullness of what God wants to pour into us through His Holy Spirit? Might we experience more fruitfulness, and in particular more progress in differentiation, if we were to open our hearts more widely to the Holy Spirit's influence in us?

Are you believing God for this good news *today*? Perhaps in the past you've trusted in His power to deliver you or strengthen you. But how about now? Are you willing to trust Him to fight inside of you for differentiation today?

Part II:
Some Practical Advice

Chapter Six:
Make Use of the Hard Stuff

Alfonso, Petr and Jennifer

"Where are we going, Al?"

"I ... I'm not really sure, to be honest. I've just kind of got a hunch."

In a panic over the newest revelation, Alfonso and Jennifer had fled Petr's church office with hardly a word to each other. They'd jumped into the car and started driving away before discussing where they were going next.

Both were consumed with anxiety now and extra words felt like a waste of their remaining energy. Petr's looming suicide suddenly seemed so much closer, and both were acutely aware that almost a day had gone by and they were no closer to finding Petr's actual location, in spite of all the clues they'd uncovered.

They were on the Interstate before Alfonso asked, "Can you read that note again Jen?"

Reluctantly, she drew it out and read:

> *Jen, I know you're probably looking for me. Please stop. You won't find me. I've gone where all my troubles started. Please know that I've always loved you and the kids. Please say goodbye to them for me.*

They were both silent for a while. Then Jen asked, "What could this mean? 'I've gone where all my troubles started'? What does that even mean, Al?"

"I'm not sure. I've just got this hunch." Al paused for a long moment and then asked, "Say, where was Svetlana's old home? You know, the place she raised Petr for most of his childhood?"

Jennifer looked surprised. "That place? Oh, that's like all the way on the other side of town. It isn't too far from the Brickyard actually. Why, what are you thinking Al? Do you think that's where we should go?"

"I'm not sure yet. I just have this feeling. I'm just trying to work something out in my head."

"Well, we've hit evening traffic," Jennifer said, stating the obvious. "It's going to take well over a full hour to get there at this point. And there's construction right now on the Beltway."

They slowed to crawl on I-465. "Right now, it'll take like almost 20 minutes just to get to I-465 southbound." She paused, then said "I tell ya', Indianapolis traffic just gets worse every year." Making small talk seemed to ease her nerves, a trick she'd learned from many years as the senior pastor's wife. People often looked to her to provide a social lubricant in awkward settings.

Alfonso grunted in acknowledgment, but the anxiety choked out his thoughts and words so he felt as though he had nothing coherent to say.

"Al, let's do this instead," Jennifer was suddenly struck with clear-headedness. "Let's get off the Interstate right up there. One of Petr's favorite coffee shops, the place where he'd go to prep his sermons away from the busyness of church, is just a couple blocks down off that exit. Besides, you need more coffee," she was in caretaker mode now, "and we'll just be wasting our time in this traffic. We'll wait it out and then zip down to Petr's old neighborhood, if that's where you really think we ought to go, once the traffic's done. Besides, maybe there'll be some clues at one of Petr's favorite hangouts." Jen wasn't entirely sure if this delay tactic was more to calm their nerves or more to postpone the inevitable.

Alfonso nodded. He also sensed a need to slow things down just a bit, and was glad to have a few more minutes without rushing into who-knows-what. He got into the lane for the off ramp. "You know, this is probably a good idea anyways. I feel like I need to talk through some stuff before you'll understand my hunch." After several minutes he said, "Promise me it's good coffee?"

"The best" she assured him. "I think."

"I mean, Petr isn't exactly a connoisseur of good coffee." The anxiety was starting to edge away at the prospect of decent coffee and just a tinge of his normal sense of humor was returning. "Whatever it was that made this his 'favorite' coffee shop quite likely had nothing to do with the actual quality of the coffee, you know."

"Despite his many other faults, Al, Petr wasn't a total imbecile when it came to quality." A little sense of humor was coming back to her too.

Al had his doubts about this, remembering some attempts Petr had made to brew coffee when they'd roomed together during seminary. He chose to say nothing about the obvious fact that Petr had never pressured Jennifer to improve her coffee- making capacities.

The moment Alfonso got his pure black coffee he began to swill it down like a man recently rescued from a self-made raft of coconut fronds in the open Pacific Ocean. Jennifer's

---

highly specialized mocha had around what seemed like eight ingredients, so they found a private table in the corner to wait for it. When her drink finally came, Alfonso took a deep breath and said, "Jen, you know we might uncover more clues if I knew more about the leadership crisis at the church."

"Yikes, that's not a very fun topic, Al."

"That stuff never is, but you can't be a senior pastor very long without having a few good leadership crises. I come by that statement from hard won experience you know."

Jen smiled wryly and began explaining how the board had been questioning Petr's every move lately. It had led to almost two years of non-stop conflicts. His effort to boost attendance by making the service shorter and more seeker-sensitive had been met with frosty discomfort. His desire to put more talented people on the worship team was equally disliked, because it was thought the move would ruin the church's "authentic" atmosphere. He had endured stronger than usual pushback for his work to purchase the property adjacent to the church so they could convert it into a teen center and gymnasium. When a contingent of members had tried to use the church for refugee relief work, Petr had gotten into quite a tangle with them over it. He had told them that the church was no place to try to do this sort of thing, explaining that they needed to preserve the building for spiritual ministry and that lots of refugees in the building might overstrain the facilities. Besides, the well-to-do neighbors would object, and Petr was loath to disturb them. This group that wanted to do refugee relief work had then complained to some board members, who had turned it into another fight to pick with Petr.

Alfonso bristled inwardly at the news of Petr's stance toward refugees. His own church was knee deep in refugee relief work and Al had come to feel very strongly about the church's role in helping them. Besides, he was amazed that Petr, an immigrant himself, felt so little compassion toward others from beyond the borders. Even though Petr hardly remembered his earliest years in Poland, Al assumed his best friend's background would have had more of an impact on his current viewpoints.

Jennifer continued. Apparently, all these incidents had frayed his relationships with the board members, and especially with the board chair. They accused him of not being collaborative and of ramrodding his agenda through the church's normal decision-making process. When Petr tried to make adjustments to his original proposals, some people questioned his honesty and integrity, saying he was a "flip flopper," with no spine. Several expressly called his overall leadership abilities into question.

Then Jennifer explained how this was impacting him personally. A couple of years of these kinds of interactions had left Petr feeling like no one supported him. He felt like he couldn't charm anybody over to his side anymore. All this had pushed Petr to begin secretly looking for work elsewhere, outside of church ministry altogether.

This last bit of information was new to Alfonso, despite his frequent communication with Petr. His curiosity was piqued, so he asked Jennifer to elaborate on the job search.

"Oh, you know, he was trying to see if he could teach at some of the local community colleges. He's also had a couple of preliminary interviews with some local companies for sales positions. Nothing's quite been sticking though."

"Wow. If anybody would make a good salesman, it would be Petr."

"I know. That's what I kept telling him. But funny thing was, he didn't seem super excited about the kind of work he might go into. He was just interested in escaping from his current job. And you know what Al, as much as I believe in the importance of church ministry, frankly, at this point, I wouldn't feel sad to leave it all behind us."

"Escape it, you mean?"

"Yeah. 'Escape' is the word he always uses. Why?"

"It's funny, because I remember that was a word he used to use all the time back on the mission field and in seminary. When a class got too hard, or a particular duty on the mission field started to get labor intensive, Petr would mumble something about 'escaping' from it..."

"What do you mean Al?" Jen wasn't sure if she was ready for more negative exposure of her husband's faults.

Alfonso was quiet for some time, thinking through numerous stories from the past. After a bit, he began to tell Jennifer that he recognized a pattern in Petr's current handling of leadership challenges at the church—one he'd seen for years. Petr regularly took the easy way out of hard tasks. He generally worked mostly for the status quo instead of for positive change.

Jennifer was a bit taken aback by these accusations. "Petr doesn't take the easy way out, Al. He has endured so much..." The defensive tone in her voice sprang up quickly.

"Now, just hear me out Jen. I'm not saying Petr is some monster. I mean, he and I have been talking about this ever since we met on the mission field. We were always debating whether the Gospel makes you tamer or wilder. I used to argue that it makes you more aggressive and bold, and he would argue that it would make you tamer, and that's how it should be. In his more humble moments, he would admit to me that he believed this because he was afraid of things getting too difficult. He would admit to me that he would always prefer to avoid hardships and challenges that couldn't be overcome with his charm."

Jennifer sighed deeply. "I guess I have to admit that I've seen and heard the same stuff too. It's just … It's just so embarrassing to see your husband wimp out on stuff."

"I never said 'wimp out' Jen. I don't think Petr is a wimp. I've seen him do all kinds of brave stuff. I just think his basic default is to circumvent hard stuff when he can. I guess all of us have this tendency. But Petr would often go into denial when encountering trials. Either he denied how bad it really was, or he avoided facing its harshness in one way or another. I remember how, when confronted with personal mistakes, Petr would change the topic, or he'd over-compensate with other things, or explain it away by blaming others."

Jennifer was looking very uncomfortable now. "I, I guess I do see all that in him too," she admitted, in a disheartened tone. "I even wonder if this tendency was partly to blame for why Petr has let the church reach this current state of leadership crisis without confronting people or naming those 'elephants in the room?'"

They both were silent a little longer as Jennifer stared off into space, letting herself really feel her exhaustion for the first time that day. Alfonso enjoyed several sips of good, real coffee.

Finally, Alfonso broke the silence. "I wonder if this is why, despite being in the midst of a neighborhood that has become so culturally and racially diverse, your church has remained racially and culturally segregated for so long?"

"Segregated? Al!" Jen said in a shocked tone, "We're not segregated! Anyone is welcome at our church. And you can't be calling Petr a racist! I mean, look. He's got *you* as a best friend!"

"I'm not saying he's racist Jen, I'm just wondering out loud. I mean, he and I have talked a lot about this for years. Your church contrasts to my church, which has seen a flourishing of its multi-cultural and multi-ethnic ethos in the last couple of decades. We've diversified as the neighborhood has diversified. But your church has remained as white as white can be."

"Hey, we have that one Asian family..." Jennifer blurted out.

"Jen, please don't get defensive. Petr and I have talked lots about it, and he says he wishes the church were more diverse. He agrees with me that church settings shouldn't be so segregated, and that your church doesn't represent the diversity of Indianapolis. But he keeps telling me that, despite the fact that people of color are always welcome, none ever seem to come."

Jennifer was starting to get annoyed now. "So, what exactly are you getting at if you're not calling Petr a racist?"

"Well, I'm just making this possible connection between Petr's tendency to find the easy way out and the lack of diversity in your church. You see, Jen, diversity takes effort—lots of effort and sacrifice and getting out of your comfort zone. My church isn't diverse just because of our location. It's diverse because we've all made huge efforts to make it that way."

"Well, so have we, Al" said Jen, her voice getting a bit sharp. "We always make a big deal about Martin Luther King Day, and Petr's on this one very diverse committee made up of inner city pastors."

"I'm not talking about that. I'm talking about how inter-racial, inter-cultural relationships require us to get out of our comfort zones. They involve putting yourself into a lot of awkward, unpleasant situations. It means making yourself uncomfortable, a lot. And I'll be the first to admit that it's just plain easier when you only have to relate to people of your own culture and ethnicity."

"Still sounds like you're calling Petr a racist."

"Hey, Jen, I'm not saying it's racist to want to relate with people like you. It's easier for *me* to relate with second and third generation

192

Latinos, but it's kind of uncomfortable for me to relate with new Latino immigrants. Even though my parents were immigrants, there's still all this awkwardness. Second and third generation Latinos all have a shared experience and culture. It's funny, but this is why it's even easier sometimes for me to relate to white people than to my own parents, who weren't raised here. You and I share more culture and experience than I share with my parents. So, I'm not talking about racism per se, even though it can turn into racism. But I think you have to acknowledge that it's more comfortable to stick with people who are similar to you."

"And I think Petr was just focused on what we *all* share together," Jen insisted. "'*All* lives matter,' you know Al."

Al judiciously chose not to take on Jen's insensitive remark in that moment. He breathed deeply again and said in as neutral of a tone as he could muster, "Maybe, Jen. But sometimes what you're saying is actually code for 'what all of us white, upper middle class people share together.' Cross-cultural ministry takes a willingness to change ourselves, and it takes a sacrifice of what we think we *should* share together."

"Oh, Al, I'm sorry but this is getting too personal. And how is any of this actually helping us find Petr? I feel like we're wasting our time here."

Alfonso paused and swallowed his last sip. "I'm sorry Jen. I truly don't mean to insult you or Petr or your church. But believe it or not, this issue does relate to this suspicion that's been growing in me for a while now."

"What's that?"

"Jen, I kind of think Petr's discomfort with cross-cultural situations has something to do with his rejection of his Polish background."

Jennifer could acknowledge this reality without getting defensive. "Yeah, I guess Petr has had a total lack of interest in integrating the best of his Polish cultural origins with the best of his adopted American culture. He just wanted to keep it all separate and never mix the two. He claims he can hardly remember anything about his early years in Poland, even though he was like eight or nine when they emigrated. And once Svetlana died, we completely stopped putting out any of those Polish Christmas decorations that were so precious to her. I've always told myself it was because he was embarrassed of Svetlana. But maybe it was more that he was embarrassed about being Polish?"

"It might have been embarrassment Jen. I don't know. But don't you think there's a similarity between his lack of connection to his Polish heritage and how Petr wants to compartmentalize all his troubles, instead of integrate them?"

Now Jennifer was quiet for a long time as she thought hard about a variety of connections going on in her mind.

Finally she spoke up, "Al, do you think Petr's motivation to please people and avoid hardships had its roots in his desire to please his mother? You know, he grew up believing that he was responsible for making his mother happy, even when her wishes contradicted Scripture."

"Hmmm," Alfonso nodded, intrigued.

"Oh, and I just hate admitting this Al, but I guess we've let all our dirty laundry spill out to you, so I guess there's no shame in it now. But I've always wondered why Petr never fully learned to prefer me, his own wife, over his mother. Almost every time there was a conflict between us, He stood up for his mother instead of for me."

"It's like Petr never did the hard work of confidently asserting himself to his mother as an adult?" Alfonso finished her thought for her.

"Yes." Jennifer sighed again and stared out into space, overwhelmed by another wave of exhaustion.

"Hey, look at us, regular psychotherapists! But seriously Jen, what we're talking about is that Petr didn't develop much of his own identity as distinct from Svetlana's approval."

"I wonder," Jennifer began, "If this was some of the reason he never knew how to stand up to the church board or to other important church stakeholders or to those neighbors as all the leadership crises began to unfold. He only knew how to relate to them in a way that was ingratiating and sort of servile. He never seemed to have a strong enough sense of his own identity to stand up for what was right.

"And this still makes me really mad, Al" Jennifer went on. "Just like your description of the mission field and seminary, Petr always found ways to sneak out of our pre-marital counseling. He even found excuses to avoid the marriage counseling sessions I insisted on about five years ago. He kept delaying for one reason or another, saying 'I've got this covered. I don't need this counseling.'"

"That's almost word for word Petr's reasons for why he didn't need to go to all the training sessions for our African mission!" Al interrupted. He'd forgotten all about that until now. "It's coming back clearly. It's almost my very first memory of him. Petr showed up just before we left for Africa, and explained to me how he'd charmed his way out of the two-month training. He had used the same phrase: 'I've got this covered. I don't need this training.' And then I remember how he used that phrase again in seminary. He said it when he charmed the dean into excusing him from one of the critical but inconveniently timed ministry internships. I mean, I love the guy, but sometimes it felt like everywhere he went, he used his charm to escape hard, boring and unglamorous training situations. I remember how he even spurned the generous offer of a more experienced, successful pastor to mentor him in his first years of the pastorate. Do you remember that, Jen?"

"Yes," she said tersely. For the moment now she was more annoyed with Petr than with Alfonso. "But Al, I still don't know how all this relates to Petr's whereabouts. We really are running out of time."

"OK, here's how it all connects Jen. All this fear of human opinion, and fear of his mother's opinion, and his tendency to avoid hard stuff; well, I think it's connected to where he might be trying to hide out until his birthday."

"OK. ...?"

"You see, he's got this unresolved thing about pleasing people, which he learned from trying to please Svetlana. His note said he was going 'where all the trouble began.' I think he sees his trouble as beginning with Svetlana. We also know he didn't bring his wallet or your credit cards with him, so that means he hasn't tried to check into any hotels. He'd have to be hiding someplace he can stay for free. So, I think he would go someplace where he can try one last time to overcome these fears that are haunting him, where 'all the trouble began.' Svetlana died before he could resolve it directly

197

with her, but I wonder if he went to the *place* he and Svetlana shared as he grew up?"

"To those old apartments near the Brickyard?" Jennifer asked. "Is that why you were asking about those earlier? Oh, Alfonso, I'm pretty sure those would have been torn down by now. They were so old and disgusting, and there's been lots of new development near the Raceway."

"They're not torn down. They're all boarded up, but they still exist."

"How do you know that?"

"This morning, when I was going over his browser history on your home computer, he hadn't erased everything. He had searched for this one address just yesterday. I checked it out, and look..."

Alfonso showed Jen a picture on his phone, "That's where he used to live, isn't it?"

"It *is*, Al" Jen said after glancing at the photo, a shiver travelling up and down her spine.

"And it's the most current Google Maps satellite picture, taken just a few months ago."

"Seems like kind of a long shot, Al," Jen began.

"Hey, it's the best lead we have right now Jen. The fact that he searched for it just a few days ago shows it was probably his destination. It's worth a shot Jen." He glanced out of the coffee shop window. "Hey, evening traffic has died way down. We could make it to the Raceway in about twenty minutes. Shall we do it?"

Now that they might be on the verge of actually finding Petr, Jen felt a wave of nausea go over her. But instead of compounding her exhaustion, the nausea gave her a strange jolt of new energy. Perhaps that was a sign, a little ray of hope? But it was also mixed with fear of what they would find.

The Hard Stuff: Hard Assignments, Experiences, Training and Relationships

In this chapter, you may have noticed a pattern in Petr's behavior; he regularly squirmed his way out of hard assignments, experiences and training. He showed a pattern of avoiding challenging relationships. He relied heavily on his charm, good looks, and exceptional talents to get him through these things. Instead of allowing these challenges to bring him to the end of himself so that God could use them to eventually transform his character, he sought to escape them most of the time.

This pattern hurt Petr later in life and ministry when his good looks were fading with middle age and his charm and talent couldn't solve problems with the same old ease. By refusing to come to the end of himself and by failing to turn to God in these earlier challenges, Petr had cultivated a pattern of avoiding God's intervention in his life. The end result was that Petr did not cultivate a differentiated self, and was therefore incapable of handling inevitable future ministry stress with resilience.

The major finding of my (Chris's) research was that leadership resilience is correlated to how a person goes through developmental challenges in life. In other words, people can become resilient leaders through hardships, *if* they go through certain kinds of hardships a certain kind of way.

Not all hardships are created equal, so just because you've experienced some hardships is no guarantee that you will become a resilient leader. Rather, the hardships we're talking about must be the kind that enables you to cultivate your biblically differentiated self. And as a would-be resilient leader, you must cooperate with God's efforts to nurture your differentiated self *while* going through the hardships.

For the rest of this chapter, we'll look at the kinds of trials and obstacles that can be the most beneficial for becoming more differentiated. My research revealed that they fall into four major categories. I tested for each of these categories. You can find a link to more information about my research at the end of this book. These four categories are: hard assignments, hard experiences, hard training and hard relationships.

Hard Assignments

My research showed that hard assignments, whether from work or from life in general, could be among the most helpful of opportunities to nurture a biblically differentiated self. In particular, I found that differentiation is most likely to occur when those assignments involve increased responsibility, or when they involve working with people from a different culture, or when they require you to implement change.

Increased Responsibilities

Increased responsibility can be a wonderful opportunity to differentiate. Think about a season in life when more was suddenly demanded of you. Perhaps it was a new job, or a new task in an already existing job. Perhaps it was marriage or parenting that foisted new standards on your behaviors and commitments. Whatever the situation, expectations of your performance were raised, and to perform at that higher level you needed to step up your game. It was likely a stressful time and one riddled with anxiety. Maybe that stress and anxiety were what you remember most about it. But it was also likely a time when you discovered that you had more in you than you previous knew. You had more competence, more inner resources, and more ability to endure than you previous thought possible.

Several things happen inside you in the face of increased responsibility that can lead to your increased differentiation. First, your created self asserts itself in previously unexplored ways. To survive and thrive, your created self rises to the occasion with formerly unknown strengths and resources. You hadn't known you could do this or that, but the circumstances demonstrate that you actually can. This assertion of your created-self can wean you off former dependencies you had assumed you needed to survive.

For instance, let's say you start a tough new job. At your old job you thought you could only do your best work when you were partnered with Tom. But in the absence of Tom, you realize not only that you can do the work but you can do it even better without Tom. The assertion of your created self frees you from over-identifying with others in a way that used to suppress your potential.

The dark side of your creative self also rises up in these situations, but even that can ultimately be a very good thing for your differentiation. As described back in Chapter Two, one's dark side includes the weaknesses and liabilities that are a natural part of being human. These can get a person into trouble if not managed well.

The key to managing one's dark side is self-awareness. And self-awareness is exactly what we have the potential to gain in a stressful situation like receiving more responsibility.

When we receive a new level of responsibility, the stress involved has a way of exposing to us and to others what we're really made out of. And it is this exposure that helps us more realistically acknowledge the dark side of our true, created self, warts and all.

As our weaknesses are exposed, we can learn to recognize them and even welcome them, rather than fight them or deny their existence. In the long run, we become better, more resilient and differentiated leaders if we can account for and manage our dark sides. This begins through the self-awareness that comes from stressful situations like new responsibilities.

Of course, many of us attempt all the harder to cover up our weaknesses in stressful situations, especially those in which our performance counts. We can be tempted to project out to others a false self, like Petr did — one that appears more competent and capable than reality. So, just because you've been handed new responsibility is no guarantee that the positive side of your created self will rise to the occasion or that you'll get more in touch with your dark side. Only the potential for this exists.

New responsibilities also have the potential, though not the guarantee, that we will cling more tenaciously to our re-created self, to God, and to His community. The exposure of our weaknesses has a way of helping us feel more acutely our need for God's truth, for His immediate help, and for the support of His people. For many of us, it is new responsibility that drives us to our knees before God, His truth, and His people in the first place. Responsibility can cause some of us to get serious with Him for the very first time. All of this can benefit our cultivation of biblical differentiation.

Working with People from a Different Culture

My research revealed that increased responsibility is not the only kind of hard assignment that can aid our journeys toward a more differentiated self. I found that working with people from a different culture is especially helpful toward this end.

You might wonder why we included this under "Hard Assignments." If you've ever worked cross-culturally, whether it's church ministry or business, government or missionary work, you know that no matter how well-meaning all parties may be, no matter how well-intentioned and no matter how positive, altruistic or rewarding, cross-cultural work can be hard.

Language barriers are only one element that makes it hard, since cultural differences go beyond language. Far subtler, and often far more difficult, are barriers that arise from culturally based values and actions like expectations of productivity, time management, and body language.

It is beyond the scope of this book to detail all the intricacies of cross-cultural work and ministry. Plenty of other good books have been written about this topic.[2] But consider for a moment how the stress of cross-cultural ministry can be an opportunity for biblical differentiation.

---

[2] See Sherwood G. Lingenfelter's books as a place to start, such as *Ministering Cross-Culturally: An Incarnational Model for Personal Relationships* (3rd ed., 2016); or *Leading Cross-Culturally: Covenant Relationships for Effective Christian Leadership* (Ada, MI: Baker Academic, 2008).

First of all, as with the previous heading, the stress can be a doorway into greater dependence on God, His truth and His people. Just as previously described, the stress of the interaction can force us to a place of searching for God's help, strength and inspiration. As we find our patience run dry with others and with different cultural norms, we turn to God for grace to be patient. When we are tempted to give up with certain people, we look to God for the grace to persevere. As we find that certain aggravating people and situations from other cultures get under our skin more rapidly than those from our culture, we look to God for forgiveness and the ability to forgive. We find we need God and His community more than before.

Second, cross-cultural situations can also be wonderful opportunities to practice relationships in which we do not already overly identify with others. When we relate with people of our own culture, the interactions can feel smooth and effortless. This means relationships can happen with little to no self-awareness. The ease can make us think nothing of becoming emotionally dependent on another, or of allowing another to become emotionally dependent on us. But cultural differences act a natural barrier in a relationship so that we do not rush too quickly into over-identification with another. Because they are not easy, we become much more deliberate and selective about how we grow close to others. It is very difficult to over-identify with another person when we have less in common and when it takes work to make the relationship successful.

This hard work in cross-cultural relationships also forces us to become more self-aware of these dependencies. When pondering our cross-cultural relationships, we might ask ourselves "why is this connection so much harder than my other connections?"

And if we are serious about discovering the answer, the question can lead to very fruitful self-awareness about why we feel close to some people and not to others. The fact is that in many of the relationships that feel close, the sense of intimacy is actually just over-identification or fusion rather than healthy intimacy.

Change-Implementing Jobs

Another hard assignment that is helpful for differentiation and resiliency is taking on a job that requires you to implement change of some sort. This means the kind of job in which you must lead a fundamental alteration in how people view things and in how they get things done. It is the opposite of maintaining the status quo, the opposite of keeping things running smoothly as they've always been run.

Implementing change demands we grow in our differentiation. Think of all the ways we depend on the status quo in the various organizations of which we are a part. Whether that organization is a business, a church, a school, a government, or a family, we often tend to over-identify with things the way they are. The status quo is often beneficial to us on a personal level, and so there is rarely a strong sense of need for change.

But even if we do not have a vested interest in the status quo, think of how all our friends, relatives, neighbors and co-workers have vested interests in the status quo. This means that our friends stand to lose if things change. And if we try to change things, we will potentially cause harm to people we love. When we over-identify with others, *their* investment in the status quo can hinder *us* from pursuing needed change.

For this reason, implementing change in an organization demands that we differentiate from the status quo. It demands that we differentiate from the people whose dislike of change might hold us back.

Whenever you begin the process of implementing change, you usually begin by asking yourself "what in me is resisting this change?" Just asking this question is the beginning of differentiation, because by asking it you inevitably discover that some of your inner obstacles are your over-identification with people and with the status quo.

Just imaging a changed future can push you toward differentiation. This is because change forces you think about whether or not you will be happy, strong and flourishing in a situation that is not this current situation. The more you can imagine being well off in a situation other than this one, the more easily you will be pried free from it and the less personal trauma you will experience from the loss of the old way.

Best of all, imagining a preferred future can make your soul overall more flexible. By this we mean that just the exercise of your imagination will enable you to move more easily from an old situation to a new one, with less distress and greater happiness.

And if you are leading the change implementation, then you will be forced to help others imagine the preferred future for themselves. This is one of most challenging but rewarding aspects of leadership. If you learn to do it well, you will help others cultivate differentiation along with you. By leading in this way, you can shepherd whole communities to grow in differentiation and therefore resiliency.

As with all the previous types of hard assignments, leading change implementation pushes you to rely on God and His truth more deeply than before, which is always a benefit.

Hard Experiences

I found in my research that there is a whole category of hardships that can be the perfect training ground for growing in differentiation and thus resiliency. We're calling this category of hard or "developmental" experiences. These experiences include persevering through perceived or real professional barriers, overcoming traumatic or emotionally laden life experiences, enduring challenging childhood experiences, and personal mistakes.

Persevering through Perceived or Real
Professional Barriers

When you persevere through professional barriers, real or perceived, your created and re-created self is forced to expand and grow. Your self-in-relation can't help but grow along with the others.

The key to differentiating by means of these trials is perseverance.

That's right—perseverance. A marathoner does not train for a marathon by sprinting short distances. She trains by slowly increasing, week after week, her running distance until at last her body is used to the 26.2 miles of the race. The ability to persevere through the marathon is gained through perseverance itself. Not other training, while helpful, adequately replaces actual perseverance.

The same is true when we persevere through professional barriers. We gain perseverance (and therefore resilience) *as* we persevere.

But what typically holds us back from persevering through professional barriers? There are internal barriers and external barriers. Let's look at in the internal barriers first.

As with implementing change, sometimes we are wedded to our current professional level because we are emotionally fused to the status quo. We sometimes inappropriately cling to and overly-identify our welfare with how things are right now. In other words, we face the same problem reiterated throughout this whole book: we're fused.

This is probably the strongest internal barrier. There are all kinds of reasons we fuse with our current position. For example, we can fear the unknown or be reluctant to pay the price of investing in perseverance. Thus, the present feels much more comfortable and a different future might just cost too much. In the same way, every day the marathon runner must face fear of injury. She must face anxiety over the loss of time and energy when she commits to persevering on a long run.

Or, sometimes we're fused to the present because of a simple failure to imagine the better future that may come through perseverance. The failure to imagine makes the present situation seem more appealing.

But if the marathoner gives in to the appeal of the present, she won't persevere. Like the marathoner we must imagine a preferable future that is different from the life we now live.

Imagining a better future helps us to let go of the present, with all its comforting limitations, and move into the unknown. The marathoner must likewise imagine a future that is preferable to the current situation in order to triumph over a great obstacle. To attain 26.2 miles, she must differentiate herself from her current self-image of a lower capacity runner.

Think of the ways your created self will benefit by discovering untapped capacities through perseverance. If you are called to advance, think of how getting a new credential or training will benefit your created self in the long run.

Like training for a marathon, the process will certainly exhaust you, and it will certainly demand some sacrifice of time, energy and probably money. But when you have persevered, you will look back and discover that your created self has enlarged in new ways that you had previously thought impossible. You will have flexed and strengthened previously unknown "muscles" in your intellect and in your skill sets. You will have expanded your "lungs" of emotional capacity. And you will discover that the very sacrifices themselves forced you to have greater self-awareness and greater wisdom in deciding what was worth sacrificing.

Best of all, by the time you have persevered through the barriers the very perseverance itself will have increased your capacity for the higher level of responsibility.

Just as the marathoner is ready for the marathon by persevering through the training, you will be ready for the higher position by persevering through the training of facing the obstacles to perseverance.

In this way, perseverance helps you to differentiate and therefore become more resilient.

And as with other challenges mentioned earlier, perseverance enriches your relationship with God and your sense of your re-created self. When we imagine a different future, anxiety arises: "will I be OK if my situation is different?" This is a normal fear that everyone must face when trying to persevere. So, in order to calm that anxiety and stabilize our sense of well-being in the face of the unknown, we must discover that, "God is a very present help in time of trouble" (Psalm 46:1). So in the same way that stressors can cause us to cling to God, the effort to persevere can cause you to cling to the God who is your very present help.

But what about the external barriers?

Some of what we imagine to be external barriers are actually internal ones in disguise. But when we do a little scratching beneath the surface, we often discover that it was primarily an internal barrier after all. For instance, one apparently external barrier might be a lack of skills or credentials. Yes, this is an external barrier. But how much of this barrier is really the result of our self-talk? It is common to tell ourselves that the necessary higher degree is too expensive and will take too much time. But are those truly insurmountable barriers that can't be overcome with some creativity and perseverance? Would they appear to be so obstructive if we eliminated the naysaying self-talk?

Take a moment to imagine that goal without all the naysaying. Think through it again without instantly sabotaging your own efforts at advancing and see what results.

But now let's say the barrier you face really is external. Let's say you face the "glass ceiling" that prevents many women and non-majority people from attaining the highest levels of status and position in the work place. How can perseverance make you differentiated and resilient when you're facing a fundamentally unfair system that is beyond your control?

One way to think about this is to consider how perseverance against injustice can mold you more into who you really are. In other words, it can mold and polish your created self in such a way that you can be shaped to be more authentically you as you emerge from the trials.

Unfair systems that refuse to change, despite your best efforts, can act like the harsh chemical agents that polish silver, or like the unrelenting stone that sharpens a knife. The very friction causes the improvement. Unfair systems can do the same for your soul, almost in spite of themselves, provided you persevere against them.

This sharpening effect is expressed in the Book of Proverbs, "As iron sharpens iron, so one person sharpens another" (Prov. 27:17). Solomon recognized that the grating, painful interactions could be potentially beneficial to the formation of your character. They can allow the real you to emerge more fully if you persevere instead of wither before them. This does not mean that unjust systems are ever acceptable. We should still work against them whenever possible. But sometimes it is not possible to make any headway against them, at least not during your short tenure. Or sometimes it is just not your calling to take on this particular injustice. It is in these cases that you are called simply to persevere.

As with all the other hard challenges named in this chapter, persevering against glass ceilings and injustices can cause you to dig your roots more deeply into the truths of your re-created self and into God Himself.

Overcoming Traumatic or Negative, Emotionally Laden Life Experiences and Challenging Childhood Experiences

Traumatic and negative, emotionally laden life experiences can be permanently devastating, especially when they happen to children. You all know and have ministered to people whose lives appear lastingly shattered from previous trauma. We're sure you've witnessed first hand the kind of ongoing damage that trauma can do to a person. And the earlier it happens, the worse and more enduring the results can be.

But we maintain that, through Christ, people who learn to differentiate through their past traumas can come out more resilient. My research demonstrated that even severe trauma could be a doorway to resiliency.

Even when trauma does not leave physical scars, it can leave deep emotional scars. Tragically, severe trauma can render a person permanently, emotionally disabled and incapable of dealing with basic life in a positive, let alone functional, way. A host of debilitating mental illnesses can originate from severe childhood traumas like neglect and sexual or physical abuse. These are illnesses like borderline personality disorder, dissociative identity disorder (formerly called multiple personality disorder), antisocial personality disorder, and crippling depression and anxiety, to name only a few. Some of these, along with the better known post-traumatic-stress-syndrome (PTSD hereafter), can also arise from traumas experienced during adult-hood.

Given the deep and intractable problems that can result from trauma, we do not claim lightly that a person can discover resiliency while going through such trials. Nevertheless, we believe that to be faithful to Jesus' message, we must make such a claim. Any person can learn to "overwhelmingly conquer" through Christ (Rom. 8:37).

To explain ourselves, and to explain it in a fresh way, we're going to start by talking about something you may not have heard much about since being in professional ministry. There is a branch of professional psychotherapy that has stumbled onto something the church has known about and used for centuries to heal trauma survivors. Professional psychotherapy calls it Narrative Exposure Therapy. The church has called it by various names, but it is essentially the same idea we explained in Chapter Three: embracing your re-created self.

Narrative Exposure Therapy is a branch of cognitive behavioral therapy. There are plenty of good articles and books you can access easily to understand it more deeply than what we share here. But essentially it is the process of re-writing your story of trauma. But in this re-writing, you recast yourself, the story's main character, as an overcomer instead of as a victim.

For a long time, many professional psychotherapists have agreed that Narrative Exposure Therapy is an effective way of treating post-traumatic-stress patients. We won't get into all the reasons for that here, but essentially it is effective because it retrains traumatized people to think, feel, and behave differently in reaction to their trauma. By retelling themselves their own story in a way that portrays themselves as triumphant versus trampled upon, they eventually re-learn to see all of life through entirely new, more positive lenses. Negative feelings and behaviors eventually follow the new story line, transforming into positive feelings and behaviors. PTSD survivors can go on to live positive, constructive lives.

What does this have to with our ideas about resiliency? It is related because professional psychotherapy has stumbled upon what Christians have been doing with their traumatic pasts since the First Century.

When a person comes to Christ, she begins the slow process of learning who she really is in Christ. She begins to tell herself His story, discovering along the way how it applies to her life and how it makes her any different or better off than she was before. She discovers over time how her identity is very different from the one that was handed to her by her family and culture and circumstances. She discovers that it is very different from the identity she may have invented for herself in her pre-Christian years.

Christians have based this idea in the passage from Romans 12:2, "Be transformed by the renewing of your mind." The end result of this transformation is the capacity to "test and approve God's good, pleasing and perfect will" (verse 2, part b). The new story the Christian tells him or herself is about being an object of God's mercy (verse 1, in reference to Chapters 1-11).

This new story is about a person created in the image of none other than God Himself. It is the story of a person created to broadcast forth His image to the universe with accuracy and attractiveness. It is the story of this same person kidnapped, through her own folly, and unwittingly made to slave away under the control of her Creator's enemy. It is the story of this Creator, so furious at the kidnapping, so delighted in the kidnapped one, that He takes the most extreme measures possible: He drastically humbles Himself, giving up His own glory, to identify Himself with His loved one, and to chase her down in the very heart of His enemy's territory. It is the story of this Creator sacrificing His very life for His lost child, atoning for her sins with own body and blood, to rescue her back from the enemy's clutches.

222

This is the story of a God who picks up this rescued child, re-adopts her as His own, outfits her in beautiful, flattering clothes, nourishes her back to health with the finest food and resources, settles her in a loving family, and trains her to co-rule over His kingdom in partnership with Him. It is the story of this God elevating this rescued former slave to the highest status possible by wedding her to Himself and living happily with her for all eternity. In short, it is the ultimate rags to riches story; the enslaved prostitute becomes the cherished daughter and the glorious queen, but at a horrific price: the very life of the King Himself.

So, in the same way that the PTSD survivor retrains his negative thoughts, feelings and behaviors by retelling himself his story, the Christian retrains himself by retelling himself the story of Christ, adopting it as his own, claiming its truth to be applicable to his own life.

This retelling in no way minimizes the severity of past traumas. Rather, it looks the traumas square in the face, seeing them for all their ugliness, and says to them "I am no longer victimized by you. You no longer determine or control my identity. I am an overcomer, 'for I am convinced that neither death, nor life, nor angels, nor principalities, nor things present, nor things to come, nor powers, nor height, nor depth, nor any other created thing, will be able to separate [me] from the love of God, which is in Christ Jesus our Lord' (Rom. 8:38)."

This is exactly the process we promoted in Chapter Three: embrace your re-created self: the new you in Christ. When a Christian embraces his re-created self, he undergoes the process of offering his traumas to God, both the ones that were inflicted upon him and the ones for which he may have been partially culpable. And he lets God re-explain their significance to him from God's perspective.

Thus, a Christian can re-interpret every trauma through an entirely new lens. For example, a debilitating injury doesn't get to identify a person as "disabled" or "weakling." Instead, the Christian gets to re-interpret the injury as having her "treasure in earthen vessels, so that the surpassing greatness of the power will be of God and not from" herself (2 Cor. 4:7). The disability takes on a redemptive interpretation rather than a broken one.

Or, instead of childhood abuse labeling one a "victim," the Christian can re-interpret it as "producing an eternal weight of glory far beyond all comparison" (2 Cor. 4:17). Instead of traumas only ending in "affliction, crushing, despair, forsaking" and "destruction" (2 Cor. 4:8-9), they can have purpose, "so that the grace which is spreading to more and more people may cause the giving of thanks to abound to the glory of God" (2 Cor. 4:15).

None of this excuses the terrible injustices and evils that are inflicted on people. Nothing ever makes atrocities like child abuse, rape, human trafficking or genocide acceptable or justifiable. But the re-telling of our own stories according to God's story turns unspeakable tragedy into triumph. The victim who is otherwise defenseless and without resource inexplicably becomes a victor in God's story. The story that would otherwise end sadly without redress of grievances or vindication of the good gets to end with righteousness conquering wrong, when we let God retell it.

Personal Mistakes

"I can trust God for growth, differentiation and increased resiliency when bad things happen *to* me," some of you are thinking, "But not when *I* am the cause of my own troubles." We know some of you are thinking that right now. "I can get through anything, as long as I didn't make it happen," some of you firmly believe.

This is quite a natural response, especially for those of us familiar with leading and being responsible for other people. After all, what is more shameful than digging our own graves? How can we call on God or on our human support systems to help us be resilient when we shoot ourselves in the foot with our own folly? If we cause our own suffering, don't we, to some degree, deserve the suffering?

We assert that even personal mistakes are opportunities to differentiate and become resilient. My (Chris's) research demonstrated this.

First of all, consider how personal mistakes force you to be self-aware. In particular, consider how they force you to be aware of your dark side. Mistakes are one of the most unpleasant ways of getting in touch with your dark side, but they are also one of the most effective. After all, it is usually a mistake that robbed us of our youthful self-delusion that we are invincible and invulnerable. As we explained earlier in this chapter, self-awareness of our dark side is a critical part of differentiation and resiliency.

Mistakes also force us to differentiate from how we think others need to see us. Pastors and other ministry leaders often feel as though their congregations will not be able to cope if they observe some weakness or personal failure. We feel as though the survival and welfare of the congregation depend on our squeaky clean image, even if that image is inhuman and unrealistic.

In many churches, this belief is actually based on truth. Even the slightest ripple on the perfect appearing surface of church leadership can cast an entire congregation into chaos. But when this is the case, it reveals that what you thought was the congregation's health was a mere house of cards, and not built on the foundation of Jesus Christ. Paul accused the Corinthians of building their church on "wood, hay or straw" (1 Cor. 3:12) that couldn't survive the revealing fire (vs. 13-15) because its members looked to human leadership (vs. 21) instead of the real foundation, Jesus Christ (vs. 11).

Many congregations today are built on a dynamic, charismatic, or hard-working leader instead of on Jesus Christ. This is a case of a congregation over-identifying with and fusing its welfare with the leader. It is a case of the leader over-identifying with and fusing his or her welfare with the congregation. And it almost always results in unrecoverable devastation for everybody, as we are sure you have witnessed or can imagine.

But recognizing our mistakes, and then using them to improve our level of differentiation, can spare us and spare our congregations from such devastation. Maybe you believe that others cannot handle seeing the real you, warts and all. If so, imagine how the sight of your mistakes will force you and them to re-evaluate the situation. Imagine how, after the initial shock, revelations of your weakness can help you see your congregation as less fragile, as more resilient than you had previously assumed, and as possessing more survival skills than you'd noticed before.

Most importantly, imagine how it will force them to look to God alone to be the perfect leader Who won't ever let them down. Mistakes will wean them off of you, a mere surrogate leader for God.

Seeing your congregation this way, and letting them see you as imperfect, will help you all discover that your welfare is not inextricably bound up with the other's. In fact, against all odds, God can sustain them if He so chooses, and He can sustain you despite your tarnished image.

Most importantly, mistakes humble you before God and make you *feel* the truth, instead of just believing it in your head, that you are a mere sinner saved by grace alone. We all have numerous self-defending beliefs that spring automatically into place the moment our consciences are troubled by a misdeed or a failure. But when that misdeed or failure results in real trouble, we are forced to own up to them. Reality pushes past the self-defenses. Few things keep us clinging to the undeserved mercy of God through Jesus Christ better than personal mistakes. This is exactly where God wants us to dwell, permanently, no matter how much you feel like your mistakes defeat you. In this way, your mistakes are a gateway into God's grace and differentiation.

Hard Training

So far, most of the examples we've described are things that happen *to* you, rather than things you choose to do. You might be wondering at this point if there is any way to nurture a differentiated and resilient self more deliberately.

In fact, my research showed that *intentionally* hard, "developmental" training is a great opportunity to improve your differentiation. By this we mean things like various trainings and special courses on interpersonal relationships, or internships, apprenticeships, or intentional mentoring and coaching that include some focus on relating with others. These sorts of opportunities can be wonderfully low-risk ways to improve your level of differentiation.

Let's say you obtain an internship at a church to learn the ropes of ministry. This affords a far bigger opportunity than what you might have imagined. Instead of just trying out direct ministry skills like preaching or discipleship or leading a team (all very important), the internship allows you to exercise your differentiation "muscles." Why? Because you are suddenly given real responsibilities and must interact with real ministry partners in a way that results in real fruit.

This forces you to think very intentionally of exactly *how* you interact with others. It forces you to reflect on exactly *why* certain of your contributions are bearing good fruit and others are not. It forces you to wonder about things like "why did I have such a strong negative emotional reaction when my co-worker said that?" and "why do I feel so anxious about this upcoming event?"

Each of the questions and concerns arising in an internship is an opportunity for more growth in self-awareness. Each is an opportunity to discover where we might be over-identifying and fusing with others. "I had such a strong negative reaction to her feedback because I've been looking to her and depending on her positive regard to make me feel good about my ministry." Or, "I reacted so negatively to his suggestion because, to some degree, I've built my sense of self on being successful in that area. His suggestion ripped a hole in that sense of self."

All reactions like these are signs of overly identifying with another person or thing. They're signs that you need to embrace more deeply your created-self, your re-created self, and your self-in-relationship with God and His community. Thus, your training is a great opportunity to discover your need for deeper differentiation.

The best thing about developmental training is that the risk is much lower than if this were your permanent position. It is far better to fail and struggle in a training situation than in a professional one in which more depends on your success.

You might be saying about now, "I'm too old to become an intern." That might be the case. But do you ever intentionally put yourself into any situation in which you are a learner instead of the expert? If you don't, it might be time to do so. There are plenty of courses and programs, even for those of you who have already earned a masters or doctoral degree, available for a person who is willing to learn. Putting yourself in the position of learner can be wonderfully eye opening about your future horizons for growth.

When you do let yourself be a learner instead of the expert, do you let the hardships involved bring you to the end of yourself so that God can build you back up His way? Or, like Pastor Petr, are you forever squirming out from under difficulties, finding shortcuts and circumventing the Cross that is embedded in that challenge?

And how do you help others navigate their internships and apprenticeships? Hopefully, you are helping to lead a church that is healthy enough and future-oriented enough that it sponsors developmental trainings of this kind.

As a part of these kinds of trainings, do you help learners reflect on their interpersonal skills as well as their "ministry" skills? Do you help them look within to discover where they might need to grow in differentiation? Are you helping your trainees grow by holding their feet to the fire when they encounter difficulties? Or do you always give them easy escape routes and cheap accountability that never demands they grow?

Hard Relationships

Relationships are in many respects the most crucial training ground for growth in differentiation and resiliency. As we have seen, relationships done well are at the heart of Jesus' plan for His people. But as we've also explained, it is our fusion, our over-identification, with other people and not simply strife and alienation that drags us down and prevents us from being resilient. Like invisible chains, our fusion with others keeps us tethered to the sinking ship of a relationship calamity. The other person's debilitating devastation becomes our debilitating devastation. The other person's favor or disfavor becomes the levers that can either switch on or switch off our sense of contentment with ourselves. Our ability to rise above and recover from disasters is dependent on the degree to which we have tethered ourselves to other people. Much of Pastor Petr's misery came from being tethered this way.

How do we train ourselves to be more resilient than Petr in our leadership? We're going to talk a lot more in a later chapter about how specifically to work on our differentiation with people. But for now, we want to emphasize that one critical way to improve your overall resiliency is to work intentionally on differentiating from those with whom you work and live. My (Chris's) research showed the necessity of this kind of intentionality.

Petr would have been spared much agony if he had learned to differentiate from his mother. He had learned to overly identify with people in his congregation by first overly identifying with his mother, Svetlana. She had trained him, certainly unknowingly, to make pleasing people his main goal in leadership. He became good at it by practicing on her, and he carried this skill into his pastoral job. It turned into his *modus operandi* with members of his congregation. His leadership came to orbit around a selfish need to charm people into liking him. People became mere tools to this end. But this approach blew up in his face when he felt he could not please a key organizational stakeholder, the chairman of the board. This man's disapproval crushed Petr. The disapproval of other congregants tortured Petr privately.

Petr missed a wonderful opportunity to differentiate from Svetlana when he married Jennifer. Marriage is intended for just such a purpose (Gen. 2:24). Instead, as Jennifer testified, Petr couldn't ever really bring himself to prefer his wife over his mother. He remained fused with Svetlana to her dying day.

In order to improve your level of differentiation, you want to take advantage of situations like marriages. They are opportunities. My research showed that people who do seize these opportunities are the people who tend to be more resilient. Unlike Petr, these are the people who engage with organizational stakeholders in a way that treats them as humans. They are not tools to exploit like Petr treated them. They are not the final determiners of your sense of self worth as Petr regarded them.

People who take advantage of relationships as opportunities to differentiate make the most of hard relationships. They seek to order them rightly so that they do not overly identify with people. They also use the hard relationships to avoid being exploited, instead of how Petr let himself be exploited by his mother for her selfish desires. They benefit and advance from the positive influence of parents and significant mentors rather than allow themselves to be parasitically drained by them.

What sort of relationships do you cultivate? Are you taking advantage of your hard relationships? Are you making the most of your connections with people in your life and in your organization?

You might protest at this point: "my key relationships are just fine. It's all these other, annoying people who make me feel stuck. What do I do about them?" Everybody has some relationships that feel annoying, irritating, or counter-productive. These aren't necessarily the people with whom you'd choose to spend time. But the obligations of kinship or of ministry demand that they be in your life. What are you supposed to do with them?

Our viewpoint is that it was God Himself who sovereignly put these irritating, draining people into your life. He did this, not to wear you out, but precisely to pin point where you need to grow in differentiation.

For example, let's say you find yourself stuck with a parishioner who only likes to complain. The moment he sees you across the sanctuary, he makes b-line to you so that he can register his new grievance, without so much as a "how do you do." Instead of just turning and running, or instead of simply finding ways to shut this person out or shut him off, this is an opportunity. For what? For you to look within and ask "*Why* does this man's complaining send me into orbit? *Why* does he feel like fingernails on a chalkboard? What is it about *me* that reacts this way?"

Or lets say it's the Christmas season, and you're at the annual big family celebration. Along comes "Uncle Bob." As usual, Uncle Bob dispenses with opening pleasantries and launches immediately into an angry rant that reflects his particular political leanings. It shuts down dialogue and all you can think of is how to get out of this. You gave up challenging Uncle Bob a long time ago, since it got you nowhere. You try to listen respectfully, knowing that your Christian witness is on the line, but inwardly all your "fight or flight" instincts are activated. You go home for another year in a row grumpy and put out because you can't believe that people with crazy ideas like Uncle Bob's are allowed out of the insane asylum! You can't stop rehearsing your irritations to yourself. Again, this is actually an opportunity. It affords an open door to ask more questions of yourself: "What is it about Uncle Bob and his views that rile me up so much? Do I feel like he is an actual threat? Why do I spend so long afterwards ruminating on the interaction? What exactly does Uncle Bob threaten?"

What are you supposed to get out of asking yourself all these questions? First, the questions force you to gain deeper self-awareness, always a critical factor when trying to grow in resiliency. Self-awareness inevitably helps you discover which of the three elements of biblical differentiation is in deficit. For instance, sometimes irritating people irritate you because they remind you of a deficiency in your created self. They might expose part of your dark side about which you'd rather remain ignorant. That's a signal that you need to drill down deeper into your created self with self-awareness, self-acceptance, and wisdom to manage it.

Or perhaps the political views of your annoying Uncle Bob feel so threatening because they look as if they could topple your beliefs about your re-created self in Christ. In other words, maybe they expose your secret fear that your security in God's love is tenuous: "If people like Uncle Bob were allowed to have more of a say in government, something could actually separate us from the love of God!" This is a clear signal from God that you need to drill down deeper into the truths about your re-created self.

Some parishioners get under your skin because they feel like real threats to how you interact with God. That annoying man who only wants to log his complaints feels like he'll prevent you from entering into an appropriately worshipful attitude in the minutes before the service. It feels as if he's going to distract you from the more important people who are eager to receive your sermon and your leadership. This is a signal from God that you need to drill down deeper into your self-in-relation with God and with others.

Now, it may very well be that your relationships with these annoying people require better boundaries. All humans can only take so much irritation at a time, and if these irritating people do distract you from your real ministry and calling, then it is appropriate and right to erect, gently but firmly, boundaries that reduce your exposure to them. Because if all your energy goes to managing your irritation, you won't have any left for what God really wants you to do.

We also would never suggest that you stay in a relationship that is genuinely harmful to you or your loved ones. There are times when real abuse and harm demand that you shut certain people out or remove yourself from all exposure to them.

However, even with good boundaries in place, you can take the irritation itself as God's direct signal to you that you have an area in which to improve your level of differentiation. Irritated? Annoyed? Put out? It is time to drill down deeper into one or more of the three areas of biblical differentiation.

The good news in all this is that your irritating relationships are God's custom-built plan for your differentiation. God has uniquely suited them just for you. The benefit of enduring this process of self-examination in difficult relationships is that you come out the other side much less stressed out and troubled by them. In other words, you come out more resilient than before.

Summary

We have seen how hard assignments, hard experiences, hard training and hard relationships can all be opportunities to grow in differentiation. If God is at work in all things, you can approach these trials as God shaping and molding you. Have you seized these as opportunities? Or, like Petr, do you squirm your way out of them, whatever the cost? This does not mean that we seek after trials. Life will bring a bounty of trials our way without our needing to look for them. But when the inevitable trials do come, will you make the most of them?

Chapter Seven:
Nurture Your Created Self

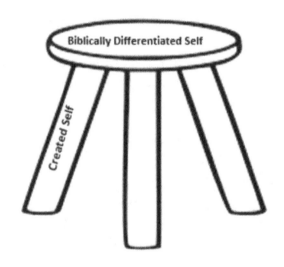

Alfonso, Petr and Jennifer

As they pulled out of the coffee shop parking lot, Alfonso felt his anxiety mount. Every mile they drove was potentially a mile closer to saving Petr. Or, it was a mile closer to a devastating ending that he refused to imagine. Al found his thoughts drifting back to a couple of his most recent email exchanges with Petr. As he reflected on them now, he was wracked with self-doubt. How could his friendship and efforts to help have been so ineffective?

He thought he'd addressed Petr's depression head on. He thought he'd brought his friend encouragement; at least Petr always responded as if he were being encouraged. How could Alfonso have been so fooled? How could Petr have hidden his real despair so well? Why hadn't he seen the signs earlier? Why couldn't he have thought and prayed harder for something more helpful to say? Was it because he'd been a bad listener? All his parishioners said he was a great listener. Even his wife said he was a good listener. How could it have come to this?

Alfonso thought he'd been so open and vulnerable about his own leadership struggles with anxiety and depression. He was certain that Petr was sure to be inspired. He naively thought Petr would to pull out of his funk eventually on his own. He remembered back to his carefully chosen words, to the hours he'd spent prayerfully crafting those recent emails, all in an over-the-top effort to give his closest friend the benefit of all his best pastoral skills. Remorsefully, Alfonso concluded that it must not have been enough.

Since Jennifer was driving this leg of the journey, Alfonso pulled out his phone and glanced back at these email exchanges with Petr. One in particular caught his eye.

Hey buddy!

I've been praying for you so much lately! I've been thinking a lot about our conversation a few days ago, and I haven't stopped praying for you for even a moment, and not just because the Colts had that horrible game last week ☹ ☺! Since we talked, I've remembered a few things that have really helped me during my times of depression. I hope you prayerfully consider them my dear friend.

And by the way, before you dismiss my words, know that this isn't just my standard pastoral advice I give my flock when they come to me for counsel. This is my best of the best stuff, my crème de la crème, reserved just for best friends ☺.

First of all, when I've faced depression, I have this practice of doubling down on celebrating who God made me to be. Instead of getting mired in my normal self-hating thoughts, I deliberately focus on the good thing God did when He created me. Yeah, I don't always feel it at first, but it sure does lift my mood eventually.

The main way I do this is to spend a lot of time forcing myself to thank God for all that good stuff. Yes, I said "force." I probably wouldn't preach it this way from the pulpit, since most of my people wouldn't like that word, but I do need to force myself sometimes.

And the next thing will sound kind of weird Petr, especially for a pastor who is supposed to be all gentle and kind with his people. But when I'm depressed, I assert myself more strongly than normal. You see, I don't know about you brother, but a lot of my depressive spells have come when I'm flooded with self-doubt and with this sense that I don't have a right to be here, that I'm some sort of an imposter in life. I remember you saying something similar to that when we were in Tanzania: feeling like an imposter at times.

In connection to this, I also assert to myself how right and good it is to enjoy the kinds of things I enjoy. You know how I enjoy gardening, running, and mystery novels? Well, I used to ignore those things when I got depressed because I used to think my depression stemmed only from not being connected with God, and that those little hobbies were distracting me from God. But I realized that those enjoyments actually brought me closer to God because it was God who gave them to me in the first place. So now I actually drill down into those fun things, rather than reject them. Doing this helps me celebrate the real me. It helps me throw off the despair that life is too bleak.

So, what I do then, right in the teeth of that self-doubt, is to kind of raise an even bigger fuss about my convictions, my purpose, my reason for existence, and my enjoyments. I kind of rehearse these truths to myself, and push myself to say, "this conviction IS important!" or, "God put me here for this reason and I refuse to leave earth until I accomplish it!" or, "This is GOOD that I'm reading my favorite author right now!"

Don't laugh Petr, but sometimes I even say this stuff out loud, alone in my office. This pushes me to choose to be confident, even if my heart is sinking away with fear and anxiety.

And this last thought (I promise this is my last thought bro. You know how long winded I can get in the pulpit, as you always used to remind me ☺) will sound strangest of all. When I'm feeling moments of relief from my depression, when I'm in a good place mentally, I actually reflect soberly on my limitations.

No, I don't mean I beat myself up. That just increases my depression. What I mean is that I sort of take a step back from myself and observe myself objectively, almost as if I'm observing someone else, and I give a long, careful look at my shortcomings. I don't do this to criticize myself. I do it to objectively say, "Yep, I struggle with this or that."

I know, this last one sounds weird to do when you're depressed, huh? But I do it for two reasons: One, it helps me figure out what contributes to my depression. You see, so many times I forget the chain of events that leads up to feeling depressed, but this objective assessment of my limitations reminds me: "yep, I need to account for my shortcomings. I need to remember that this or that is a weakness for me." Now, I don't do this when I'm actually depressed. That'd be stupid, because the depression would just color everything and distort my negative feelings so that my limitations appear even bigger than they are. I can't be objective while I'm depressed. But I still need to do it.

The second reason I do it is that I've found time and time again that I actually tap into God's strength in an unexpected way when I face my own darkness and soberly admit to its reality. It sort of quiets me and grounds me to get an honest look at myself. And strangely, whenever I do this, God gives me a fresh reminder of His grace in my life. It comes to me with this renewed vigor.

I don't know if this last bit makes any sense Petr, since most peoples' (including my own) natural inclination is to ignore their weaknesses when they're depressed. But if I can do this in my sunnier times, this seriously helps when the darkness comes sweeping back in.

And all this stuff I'm saying Petr helps me even when I'm not depressed. Celebrating God's work in me, thanking Him for the gift of myself, asserting myself, and taking

*stock of my limitations, it's all part of
my little recipe for emotional survival
as a pastor.*

*I'll stop now Petr. Please
know that I feel your pain. I'm
praying for you, and cheering you on.
When I'm at little Lorenzo's next
soccer game and cheering him on,
know that I'll be secretly cheering you
on too in my heart. That's how God
thinks of us. He's cheering you on,
rooting for you bro.*

*Love you man,
Al*

Alfonso stared at the screen for several
minutes. What had he missed in that letter? How
had it not gotten through to Petr's heart?

Petr's response had been terse: *Yep.
Thanks for the uplifting thoughts. Good ones. You're
the best. Give my love to Bonita and the kids. Petr*

Alfonso now realized with a sinking
feeling that nothing in his letter had gotten
through to Petr.

Nurture the Created Self

The previous chapter gave lots of insight into how we might make use of developmental assignments, experiences, training and relationships. My (Chris's) research showed that if we go through these four kinds of hardships with a conscious effort to grow from them and to use them to expand our differentiation and to break the bondages of fusion, then we are more likely to become resilient leaders when we face future hardships. But we would be remiss if we ended the book there. These last three chapters are dedicated to specific ways for you to nurture the three parts of your biblically differentiated self. This chapter is full of practical tips for how to nurture the created self.

Tip One: Celebrate and Enjoy Your Created Self

The first and possibly most important piece of advice for nurturing your created self is to celebrate and enjoy its every aspect. This means to acknowledge and rejoice in all the positive elements of who and how God has created you to be, receiving them all as gifts that God has intentionally given you in His wisdom and care. It means to meditate on and enjoy all the facets of your created self by taking child-like delight in each one as you wonder at the Creator who generously gave them to you.

Many of us must make a real effort to do this. We are so used to not doing it, that we must do it with intention and conscientiousness, even to the point of creating an actual list of our reasons to celebrate. This list distinctly enumerates each element of the created self that sticks out as celebration-worthy. Many of us must learn to pull out this list deliberately and rehearse it on a regular basis, in order to remind ourselves how we are "fearfully and wonder-fully made" (Ps. 139:14). When we do this, we affirm along with the Psalmist that "the lines have fallen to me in pleasant places; indeed, my heritage is beautiful to me" (Ps. 16:6).

We've got to be deliberate about doing this because three things can tend to swallow up self-awareness of our created selves: fear of pride, shame and comparison.

Fear of Pride

Pride is a real enemy of our souls, and we must be vigilant against it. But some of us try to fight it by fearing it, and the fear of it, if overdone, can oddly prevent us from receiving God's gift of the created self. A lot of well-meaning Christians worry that rehearsing their unique gifts is a doorway for pride to sneak in. But sincerely celebrating the created self is not a gateway to pride. Rather, it is a counterweight to it. How is this possible?

Celebrating and enjoying the created self counteracts pride because it attributes its source to God. When we celebrate and enjoy, we credit God with the intelligence, the wisdom, the kindness, and the generosity for forming and shaping us to be who we are. We in essence say "good work God! Congratulations, for all the ways you've made me. You are truly wise, and my existence is evidence of this truth." This gives real pride no room to breathe. It suffocates pride with truth.

Truth about the created self is an antidote to pride because pride is by definition a deception. Specifically, it is self-deception in which we exalt ourselves out of proportion with our real significance to God. Pride is like saying, "God made me royalty (1 Pet. 2:9), but I deserve to be the Emperor." Is it not exalted enough to be royalty? Why must we grasp after the most exalted royal position of all, a position reserved for the King of kings? Pride is akin to narcissism, which places oneself at the center of the universe in importance and imagines oneself as deserving of worshipful attention.

In contrast, celebration of the created self says, "I am satisfied with this royal position. It suits me well. God, you were wise and you did a good job granting me this exalted status. Thank you for exalting me beyond what I deserve." In fact, celebrating the created self cultivates humility, which can be defined as an *accurate* assessment of self, versus an assessment of self that is *lower* than what God has assigned it. False humility (just pride in disguise) projects a false image of being especially low in significance in God's eyes. Rehearsing our lowliness is usually part of a brazen effort to fish for compliments from God and from others. When we say, "I'm so bad at this," we're secretly hoping to hear God or someone else assure us of the opposite.

But whenever we celebrate and enjoy our created self, we move a little closer to seeing ourselves with the accuracy of true humility. True humility does not need exaggerated lowliness to thrive. True humility breeds in an atmosphere of true and accurate self-assessment. This is an atmosphere in which a person does not need to overcompensate for insecure feeling about himself through self-aggrandizement (what we normally deem to be pride), nor through self-hatred (what we normally imagine to be humility). Humility rests contentedly with exactly how and what God created you to be. Humility is satisfied with nothing more or less. Humility says, "God, *You* did well when you made me."

So, it's true that pride is an ever-present threat. It seeks any opportunity to creep in and take over a soul. But it cannot be fought with false humility. It cannot be fought by failing to celebrate and enjoy the created self. Fear of pride can actually rob us of one of the most important gifts God has granted us: ourselves. We rightly fear being engulfed by the power of pride. But we must also discern carefully between real pride and enjoying the gift of ourselves to the glory of God.

Shame

Others find it hard to celebrate their created selves because they have such a strong sense of shame regarding their dark side. In their minds, their dark side (both real and imagined) outweighs their ability to enjoy what God has done in them. And shame can be a powerful force for shutting down God's work in us. Whenever something worth celebrating of the created self rises up to the level of consciousness, shame can immediately push it back down, eliminating our awareness of it: "Yes, that was an OK accomplishment, but it doesn't negate the fact that I struggle with this other thing..."

Shame can prevent us from even a begrudging acknowledgment that something is good in our lives. It can drive us straight to a negative outlook before a positive one has had even a chance to grow. It can cause us to completely pass over any good in our lives for which God deserves credit, and it can plunge us right into despair over our sorry state.

This is a little bit like a person who can't see a delicious, mouth-watering Thanksgiving meal with all the fixings set before her. Instead, she spends the whole time dwelling on the terrible meal she had yesterday. Shame clouds out the feast of God's goodness in one's life, and causes us to dwell on reasons to despair about ourselves.

As with false humility, this response to shame can be like the attempt to fish for compliments. But instead of fishing for compliments, we fish for reassurances that God won't embarrass us again with all these unacceptable parts of ourselves.

Our shame reactions can sort of be like trying to hold God hostage: "God, I'll credit you with goodness once you erase all these embarrassing parts of myself, so that I'll never again be crushed by them." But unlike false humility, shame shrouds us in such a cloud that we are generally unaware that we are fishing for these reassurances.

The answer to shame should not be to avoid celebrating yourself. This is the response of many when they feel shame rise up in them. Many of us fear that celebrating ourself will only increase feelings of shame because it will just point out to my consciousness and to the world all the ways I don't measure up. This is a little bit like when a school child who struggles in one subject avoids celebrating another subject that she's good at because she thinks that acknowledging the good subject will demonstrate her lack of ability in the first subject. But the end result of this is a vicious cycle of self-defeating discouragement. The student's reticence to celebrate one subject just re-enforces her idea that all of school is a struggle to her.

The answer to counteracting shame is to celebrate yourself, in the very face of shame-inducing evidence to the contrary. The moment you become aware of those areas over which you feel shame, that is precisely when you want to celebrate your strengths with the greatest vigor. This will feel awkward at first, but eventually, the more you practice it, the more delight you will take in the secret celebrations going on between just you and God over His gifts in your life.

Comparison

Comparison is of course a twin sister of shame, working in tandem with it. Shame usually has the greatest occasion to run free and unhindered when we compare ourselves with others. When we compare ourselves to others and find ourselves lacking, shame is one of the most common responses to well up inside of us.

Comparison has its own unique way of squelching joy in our created self (and therefore joy in our Creator). Comparison with others is based on a false set of standards. "She's better off because she is thinner than I am," "He's better off because he bigger muscles than I do," "They're better off because they have more money than I do." "She's better off because her job title sounds fancier than mine."

All these statements, and the 1,000s of others like them, are based on false standards of measurement. It is like trying to measure the length of a piece of wood with a measuring cup instead of a tape measure. The measuring cup was intended to measure volume, not length.

But if we try to use the cup it will only leave us self-deceived and frustrated. It is no wonder this wrong standard of measurement damages our ability to enjoy. Comparison with others is an inaccurate measurement and God never intended us to use it against ourselves.

Comparison at best ignores and at worst belittles the real standard against which God calls us to measure ourselves, Jesus Christ. John writes that we are to "walk in the same manner as He [Jesus] did" (1 John 2:6), and Jesus Himself commanded that His disciples imitate Him in service (John 13:14-15) and love (John 13:34). Paul commands us to imitate Jesus' attitude (Phil. 2:5). When we compare our looks, our jobs, our homes, our incomes and so on, to other people, we get distracted from God's agenda for our lives. His purpose is that we increasingly reflect the image of God in Christ (2 Cor. 3:18). He only cares that we measure ourselves against this one Person. But this measurement appears twisted in our eyes if we believe our measurements against others are more important or real.

Comparison also wrongly forces us to discard one person's uniqueness and his special contributions in favor of another person's uniqueness and special contributions. This is like comparing a hammer to a flower. The two contribute to our lives in completely different ways, and we should not discredit the one because it is not doing the other's job. It would be like discrediting the uniqueness of Einstein's contribution of the theory of relativity by saying "Yeah, I guess his theory of relativity is OK, but compared to Planck's theory of quantum mechanics, it's pretty shabby." Both Planck's and Einstein's theories are utterly invaluable to contemporary physics and engineering, and discarding one in favor of the other would be the height of foolishness. God created each of us with vast differences, but none of these differences negate the treasure-worthiness of each person. Like both theories of physics, we can't do without the contribution of a single person's created self.

Worst of all, comparison keeps God from getting the glory for creating us. How can God get credit for His creative genius if we constantly imagine ourselves, His creations, as coming up short next to others? We can't conclude that God is wise and loving if we regularly find some people (including ourselves) to be less significant than others. It would be as if the Mona Lisa painting were to speak up when Leonardo Da Vinci were praised for her creation and say, "Well, he was OK, but did you take a look at my flaws in comparison to his other works?"

And when it comes to our own happiness, comparison imprisons us in misery. If we see ourselves as precious and treasure-worthy based on how we measure up against other people, we will sadly always find reasons to conclude that we are deficient. But if we are precious simply because we are creations of a genius God, we will always have a reason to be content.

Summary

When we fail to celebrate and enjoy our created selves, we inevitably open the door to real pride, shame and comparison. These three things can tend to swamp our personalities and dominate our outlook on life. Worse yet, they conspire to prevent us from experiencing all God would have us experience. Whenever you suppress the truth about the delightfulness of your created self, you invariably suppress the truth that God is wise, powerful and kind for having made you. The more we contemplate and delight in the numerous facets of the jewel that is our created self, the more the Creator gets credit for His genius in creating us. Our beauty and preciousness reflects the beauty and preciousness of our Creator. So, this failure to celebrate creates a vacuum, and pride, shame and comparison are only too happy to fill it.

Celebrating and enjoying your created self is the first and possibly the most important step in nurturing the created self. When you can rest satisfied with the person God created you to be, the good, the bad and the ugly, you pour cement around a secure self that does not need to fuse with other people in order to parasitically suck life from them. You go a great distance toward avoiding fusion with others that could drag you down when disaster strikes.

Tip Two: Give Thanks for Your Created Self

Closely related to the previous piece of advice is the intentional practice of gratitude. This is when we pause and say "thank you" to God for all the aspects of the created self. One of the most important and concrete ways of celebrating the created self is to make a deliberate expression of thankfulness for each and every part of you. The Psalmist, when he discovered that he was "fearfully and wonderfully made," reacted by saying "I will give thanks to You…" (Ps. 139:14).

When you express gratitude, you create a tiny little oasis for your soul in the middle of the otherwise bleak and punishing desert of this world. In this moment of gratitude, with life's harsh desert still very much in sight, you give your soul this little bit of relief, a moment when your soul can breathe in the fresh oxygen of God's grace and drink in the cool water of God's reality. You let the truth of God, that you've been "fearfully and wonderfully made," that "the lines have fallen to me in pleasant places," invade you and leaven up the dull, lonely, even miserable reality you are experiencing in the moment.

Every expression of gratitude is a savoring, however briefly, of the truth that God's reality is actually more real than the inhospitable reality of the world around you. You're saying to your soul and to the world, in effect: "No, I remember that God's goodness trumps this forlorn desert of life. This is what's really real."

A practice of gratitude helps you nurture your created self, and thus cultivates a differentiated and resilient self, in three main ways. First, gratitude certifies in your own mind that indeed, the gifts of God are good. We are often ambivalent about the gifts of God, indecisive whether they are really good for us or not. But when we express genuine gratitude for something, it forces us to make a decision in favor of the goodness of the gift. It demonstrates that we've made up our minds, "yes God, this gift from you really is good."

When we fail to thank God for His gifts, it is like when we hem and haw around saying a definitive "thank you" for that horrible gift we got last Christmas from Great Aunt Bertha. "Did you like the porcelain statuette of the mating mole rats I sent you for Christmas? I never got a thank you card," Great Aunt Bertha asks. "Ah, well, um, you know, it sure was unique," we dodge. Our ambivalence will of course communicate our disapproval of the gift. It is the same when we fail to thank God deliberately. Like celebrating and enjoying the created self, saying thank you for the goodness of the gifts reflects on the goodness of God. We can better see God as good because we see His gifts as good. And a person who is confident in God's goodness has no need to fuse herself inappropriately to another person in an effort to find life and sustenance for the soul.

Second, gratitude opens your heart to God's further work in your life. The Psalmist writes, "Enter His gates with thanksgiving..." (Ps. 100:4). There is a way in which gratitude mysteriously swings wide open the "gateway" to encountering God more deeply and fully.

When we give thanks, it is a "Yes" to God, an affirmation that God's gifts are in fact good and right. Saying, "yes, I enjoyed that" once makes it easier to experience another gift of God's. It makes our hearts more open to what God might want to do next in our lives on a deeper level.

Third, thanksgiving glorifies God. The Psalmist explains, "I will praise God's name in song and glorify Him with thanksgiving" (Ps. 69:30). Gratitude puts the Giver of gifts in a positive light. It shows Him off as praise- and honor-worthy. When we give thanks to Him, God is shown to be good.

All this enables us to be more differentiated from others and more resilient in difficulties. This is because, if we can see God as more good and glorious than we saw Him previously, the more likely we are to look to Him and not to others to be the answer and provision to our every need. Instead of over-identifying with others and inappropriately and parasitically latching on to them to draw life from them, we will look to God. Instead of feeling threatened when they disagree with us, we will more likely trust this good and glorious God to protect us from threats. And being more open to God's future work in our lives will also tend to turn us toward Him instead of toward others to meet our needs.

As a practical matter, it is fine to start giving thanks generally ("thank you God for a capable mind. Thank you for my current level of health"), but if you really want to reap the benefits of gratitude, it behooves you to get as detailed as you possibly can. The more detailed the better. How specifically has your capable mind benefited you, your ministry and those in your circle of influence? How specifically has your current level of health proved to be a blessing to others? What have you been able to do because of it? How have the lives of others improved because of it? Which parts of your health? How has it benefited you *today*?

Perhaps you'll object: "my health isn't so good. I struggle with some very serious health challenges." But are other parts of your body working well enough to keep you going in other respects? Thank God for what *is* working. Something in your body and brain must be working well enough for you to digest this much of this book. Perhaps an illness kept you from work last month, and you even lost some pay because of it. But are you functional enough that you were able to go to work *today*? Thank God that you got to go to work and earn a paycheck *this* month.

Deliberate thanksgiving will cement into your soul your enjoyment of God's work and your enjoyment of His glorious genius for how He's made you.

———
267

Tip Three: Assert Yourself

Asserting yourself is a key part of nurturing the created self. God created each part of you with intentionality and with wisdom. He did so with the expectation that all of you would get expressed and that all of you would have an influence on His church and on this world. When you assert yourself, you ensure that your created self will be expressed. You ensure that all of you will be influential, as God intended. Our created self has dignity simply because we bear the image of the Creator. For this reason and this reason alone, a person's created self is worth a kind of self-respect that requires us to assert ourselves.

By asserting yourself, we mean being *insistent* about advancing your opinions, your concerns, your beliefs, your convictions, your values, your preferences, and even your attractions and interests. At least, we mean being insistent about all the things that are in accordance with God's will.

Some of you might object at this point by asking, "As disciples of Jesus, aren't we supposed to assert *His* plan and agenda, not ours?" Jesus' agenda is most certainly our highest priority. But insofar as His agenda and plan are expressed *through you*, asserting yourself is asserting God's plan. Insofar as *you* were intended to be God's agent on earth, your self-assertion is one way in which God makes "His appeal *through* us"(2 Cor. 5:20).

In the Book of Acts, Luke gives us little glimpses into how the early church worked out this idea in practice. For instance, he records how the early church arrived at the decision to better include new Gentile converts. The letter of the apostles and church elders explained their decision-making process this way: "It seemed good to the Holy Spirit *and to us* ..." (Acts 15:28). This phrase summarizes the back-and-forth dialogue between church leadership and the Holy Spirit over this issue.

The dialogue began as a "sharp dispute and debate" at Antioch between Jewish Christians and Paul and Barnabas (vv. 1-2). So, the Antioch church referred the problem to the leadership of the Jerusalem church, who first listened carefully to Paul and Barnabas's testimonies of God's work among the Gentiles (vv. 3-4 and 12). Then they allowed those of the party of the Pharisees to make their case for Gentile circumcision and adherence to the Mosaic Law (vs. 5). They followed that up by "much discussion" (vs. 7), and then let Peter rehearse his earlier role in the conversion of Cornelius's family (vv. 7-11).

Then Paul and Barnabas were given one more chance to remind everyone of the obvious work of God among the Gentiles (vs. 12). Finally, James summarized all their concerns (vv. 13-14) and brought in the Old Testament prophetic witness on this matter (vv. 15-18). James concluded with "It is *my* judgment, therefore..."

This story paints a picture for us of the manner in which the church partners closely with the Holy Spirit for discernment. The church prays, consults Scripture (vv. 16-18), and dialogues with each other (vs. 7), allowing for a variety of apparently contradictory voices. Church members keep their eyes open for signs of the movement of the Spirit (vv. 4, 8-9, 12). Sometimes the dialoguing is full of contention (vv. 1-2), but overwhelmingly it is marked by a sense of welcome for one another and for the voices of all, just as the church leadership "welcomed" Paul and Barnabas (vs. 4) as "dear friends" (vs. 25).

This kind of group discernment requires that individuals assert themselves. They would not have understood God's direction if many of the voices had kept silent—if many had decided not to assert themselves. This particular decision required the whole church at Antioch to speak up, for Paul and Barnabas to speak up, for Peter to speak up, for James to speak up, and for there to be "much discussion" (vs. 7). It even required the Pharisees among them to speak up, because if they hadn't, the issue would never have been clarified, and the church would forever wonder if Gentile converts were some kind of second class Christians. On this issue the community had to go through a process in which they could confidently say afterwards that "It seemed good to the Holy Spirit *and to us...*" (vs. 28).

If you do not assert yourself, if you do not speak up, if you fail to celebrate your created self in the Christian community, you will fail to contribute to the group dialogue that is necessary to discern God's direction. Today God continues to present thorny situations to the church in which careful group discernment and "much discussion" are needed, even among apparently contradictory views, so that in the end the community can say confidently "It seemed good to the Holy Spirit *and to us.*"

We'll tackle the idea of asserting your convictions and values first. When a person asserts a deeply held conviction, she is likely giving expression to a value implanted by God Himself. We should say first of all that of course, there is great danger when you assert your convictions. It is quite possible to have a deeply held conviction that was not implanted by God.

When you assert yourself over something that is not from God, you are likely to do great damage and lead others astray in the process, since many will follow your passionate conviction simply because it is presented passionately and not because it is aligned with God's will. Christian leaders especially must always thoughtfully subject all their convictions and opinions to Scripture. Each must do the exacting work of discerning whether or not one's convictions show fidelity to God's revealed will.

But when you know that certain opinions and convictions really are from God you must give them expression, or risk unfaithfulness to God.

If you were raised with a certain picture of humility, it is going to be hard to assert yourself. Many have absorbed the idea that humility means a quiet, even a shy or retreating, demeanor that acquiesces quickly to others, regardless of the cost to oneself or to the truth. Many Christians have this picture of meekness that prevents people from asserting themselves.

But is this picture of meekness biblical? Let's take a look at the person the King James Version of the Bible famously describes as "very meek, above all men which were on the face of the earth" (Num. 12:3): Moses. Was Moses shy and retreating when he faced Pharaoh and demanded of him: "Let my people go!" (Exod. 5:1). Was he shy and retreating when he had to rebuke or discipline the Israelites (Num. 14:41-43, 16:5-17)?

Did Jesus fit the traditional picture of meekness? He was certainly gentle with the sick, the ashamed and the repentant. But was He shy and retreating when He turned over tables and drove out moneychangers from the Temple (Matt. 21:12, Mark 11:15, John 2:14)? Was He shy and retreating when He called the Pharisees "you hypocrites" (Matt. 23:13, 15 & 23), "You blind fools" (vs. 17), and "whitewashed tombs" (vs. 27) to their faces? Was He shy and retreating when He got ready to suffer on the cross: "and what shall I say? 'Father, save me from this hour?' But for this purpose I came to this hour. Father, glorify Your name!" (John 12:27-28)?

Was Paul shy and retreating when he warned the Corinthians that in his upcoming visit he might need to be "bold" in setting some people straight (2 Cor. 10:1)? Was he shy and retreating when he wrote his letters, letters that many acknowledged to be "'weighty and forceful'" (2 Cor. 10:10) and evening "frightening" (2 Cor. 10:9)?

Asserting convictions and values frees the Christian leader from the danger of being a chameleon. The chameleon approach to life is the fastest way to become inappropriately fused with others. If, like a chameleon, you shift your color in order to win yourself human favor in the short-term, you'll end up over-identifying with the opinions and convictions of others. This will prevent you from bouncing back with resilience when, like Petr, you find yourself unable to win human approval.

It is quite common in worldly models of leadership for leaders to express themselves only in so far as they follow the direction of the prevailing political winds at the moment. Unfortunately, Christian leaders fall into this trap all the time. And it's hard not to do so. Your salary is dependent on the church board's thumbs up. Your overall sense of success or failure is dependent on the kind of weekly feedback you get from the sermon. As a church leader, you are constantly dealing with human opinions and their fickle approval or disapproval.

But true Christian leadership, in the model of Jesus Himself (John 12:27-28) involves a dedicated march in a single direction, unswayed by the fickleness of those you lead. It requires an inner toughness, marked by a steely faithfulness to your calling. Whatever the opposition, whatever direction the winds of human favor seem to be blowing for the moment, Christian leadership requires you to persevere in the direction God gives you to pursue. It requires you to assert yourself.

Asserting your convictions and values will strengthen your created self and reduce the temptation to be a chameleon. This in turn will enable you to differentiate from others and to be resilient in crises.

Asserting your deeply held convictions and values might already be self-evident to you. After all, if you lead a church, you need to express your convictions all the time. But have you ever considered the importance of asserting your preferences, hobbies and attractions? Petr had suppressed these parts of himself for years. Perhaps it started out innocently enough for him, in a sincere effort to be "become all things to all men, so that I may by all means save some" (1 Cor. 9:22). But gradually, he'd discarded any innocent pleasure or enjoyment that had allowed him to relax, recover and refresh his soul (his motorcycle, golf, the gym, puzzles and so on). This left him with no margin in life. It proved crushing to his soul in the long run.

This is a fairly common problem among Christian leaders. Many Christian leaders feel enormous guilt for "leaving their post" for even a moment to go bowling or to indulge in a fun, non-spiritual novel. After all, that's time they could be visiting the shut-ins or preparing better for the next sermon.

Others simply get swept away easily by the busyness that is an inherent part of professional ministry. They don't realize they've lost touch with their created selves until it is too late.

Certainly there are seasons when there just isn't a Saturday that's entirely free for a luxurious game of golf. And there are seasons of fasting from specific enjoyments because the Holy Spirit is trying to break you free from the danger of idolizing those enjoyments. But to nurture the created self and to honor all God has done in creating you to be uniquely you we must learn to assert our innocent preferences and enjoyments. We must learn to give them full expression when such an expression does not pollute your own soul or when it does not exploit, neglect or damage others or dishonor God.

Asserting yourself in these matters will give much needed margin to your life, and, like regular thanksgiving, will make you feel like your otherwise burdensome life is infiltrated with oases of fun and pleasure. Part of Petr's misery, and his constant yearning to escape his "unending nightmare," stemmed from his view that life itself was entirely harsh and bleak. To Petr, life had become all grinding work without reward. If he had been asserting the enjoyable side of his created self, perhaps he would have felt as if, even though ministry itself might be unrewarding for a season, God still cared about him enough to grant him sweet little pleasures in other parts of life.

The assertion of your preferences and personal interests will make you more differentiated and thus more resilient. Many times we fuse ourselves to others because we are out of touch with what God created us to enjoy. If you've lost touch with the fact that gardening and spending time outdoors brings you joy, some needy part in you will glom on to another person's enjoyments. This will leave you parasitically feeding on others, which is a setup for over-identifying with them. But if you assert your enjoyments, you will have no need to grasp after the life inside other people. You will experience God's life inside of you. Resiliency inevitably follows.

Christian leaders especially must learn to assert both their convictions and their innocent enjoyments if they hope to become differentiated and resilient. Leaders stand in greater danger than non-leaders of dragging others down with them when they stumble and choke on their own misery. Conversely, leaders have great potential to inspire others to resilience when they themselves are resilient.

The more you assert yourself, the better you'll get at doing it. And the better you get at it, the more likely you are to become more differentiated and resilient.

This is because every time you choose to assert yourself you will strengthen your ability to stand on your own two feet, so to speak, in your convictions and preferences. It is like exercising a secret muscle of the soul. The stronger this "muscle" becomes, the less you will feel the need to fuse yourself inappropriately to other people to find validation. Instead, you become *self*-validating under God.

Self-validating does not mean being self-centered. It doesn't mean determining truth by yourself. By "self-validating" we just mean that your conviction of God's truth does not change based on the validation or disapproval of other people. People can disagree with you and you can respond by quietly assuring yourself, "this really is the truth. It is right for me to cling to this truth or to this enjoyment." You learn to exercise the judgment God gave you to approve of His ways and of His creation for yourself, without respect to human approval or agreement.

None of this talk about asserting ourselves means being inflexible in our opinions. It doesn't mean that we can't learn new things. There are plenty of Christians who are highly opinionated but whose passionate advocacy for their own views bears no resemblance to God's views about those same topics. This kind of strong "conviction" just leads to an unwillingness to learn, even from God. Rather, we're talking about a kind of self-assertion that is free of needing the approval of others to be solid and lasting.

You will find countless opportunities to improve your ability to assert yourself. If you're not used to doing it, it may feel unnatural at first. It might even feel like a violation of the kind of "humility" and "meekness" you've been taught. But you'll gradually get better at it if you practice, just like your body will get stronger if you train it.

One important practice is to learn how to assert yourself especially in the face of contradiction. When people disagree with your beliefs, practice disagreeing back. This doesn't need to be done with rancor and acrimony. It can be done respectfully and even lovingly. It doesn't even need to be done out loud. If it would be inappropriate to the situation to disagree publically, it can be done inwardly. It can be a secret self-validation as you remind yourself "it is good for me to hold this viewpoint that contradicts theirs."

And when someone disparages or disapproves of a pastime that's brought you much life and joy, practice validating your own enjoyment of it. As a word of caution, it makes even less sense to do this out loud, since it is unlikely that life and death hang in the balance.

But do it by yourself anyways. Validate your enjoyment especially when others hint that your preferences and enjoyments are signs of your inadequacy ("he just likes to golf because he's can't handle a more competitive sport"). Respond by telling yourself the real reasons you love to play golf.

In short, choose to be confident in the assertion of your convictions (if in fact they are in agreement with God), and choose to be confident in the assertion of your enjoyments (if in fact they are innocent and free from idolatry). Be wary of messages about your inadequacy and be quick to embrace the inherent goodness of your created self.

Is there great danger in this advice? Most certainly. It is not difficult to overdo this self-validation. It is easy to cross quickly into over-confidence, which can be highly damaging to the community you lead. Our resident narcissism is normally looking for any opportunity to rear its ugly head. Nevertheless, for the perennially under-confident among us (which includes a lot of pastors), asserting your created self is an important exercise, even if you get the balance of it wrong the first few times.

Now for those of us with a tendency to be over-confident, read this next tip closely.

Tip Four: Account for Your Dark Side

At first, this tip is going to sound like a contradiction to the first three tips for nurturing your created self. But don't give up reading.

We wrote a lot about your dark side back in Chapter Two. We described it, not as your "sinful nature," but as your weaknesses and the liabilities that are a natural part of being a human. We made the case in that chapter for your desperate need to account for your dark side.

Alfonso wrote to Petr that accounting for his dark side helped in two ways. First, it enabled him to connect the dots about what exactly led to his own depressive episodes. Second, it increased his sense of dependence on God's grace, which in turned helped him tap into that grace more deeply than before.

It is critical that you develop your capacity to connect the dots about your dark side. Whether it's because of shame or because of sheer ignorance, most of us don't understand how our weaknesses and limitations can be liabilities for us and for others.

Even when we experience negative consequence after negative consequence resulting from our dark side, we rarely figure out why and how our dark side works. Why am I so prone to fits of anger? What's behind my lack of administrative ability? How do I keep making this same sort of mistake? The more you can connect these dots, the better you'll become at managing your dark side, and the less of a liability it will prove to be.

So double down on your efforts at self-awareness. Notice repeated negative patterns in your life ("This same bad thing happened to me again," "I gave in to that temptation again," "Once again, I did not stop myself from overeating that dessert"). Notice negative emotions as they rise up ("I feel anxious again," "I felt so depleted after I read about that incident in the newspaper," "These political events stir up my anger"). Observe yourself and your dark side like Alfonso did, as if you were an outside party.

When you do this kind of self-observation, avoid jumping to judgment and self-condemnation too quickly. It may very well be a bad thing, and it might be worthy of condemnation. But you'll lose the opportunity to evaluate it thoroughly and helpfully if you judge it too quickly. If you judge too quickly, then all your self-justifying and self-excusing tendencies will leap to your conscience's defense. They'll shout a hundred excuses in your brain and drown out any hope of connecting the dots. Then you'll never get to the bottom of it.

Instead, step back and just observe it for a while. Try to be objective about it. Turn it around and look at it from various angles, as if you were conducting a scientific experiment on it. Even use objective, non-judgmental language when you describe it to yourself: "It's so *interesting* that I reacted that way," "It's *fascinating* that my emotions were so big over that incident," "I'm curious why this keeps tripping me up." These calm, objective observations will allow you to penetrate more effectively the mysteriousness of the emotions because they'll help you lower you defenses. This approach will allow you to connect those dots.

Still without judging or self-condemnation, ask yourself gentle questions about the phenomenon. Be curious about it: "Is there anything similar between this time and my other bouts of anxiety?" "I wonder if my anger over this is at all related to the other things that make me angry?" "The last time I felt this discouraged, I had been doing this other activity. Could there be a connection?"

If you can prayerfully and patiently follow your curiosity without self-condemnation, you can trust that the Holy Spirit will eventually lead you to connect the dots so that you better understand your dark side. This self-understanding is the first, most critical and necessary element of self-control.

Alfonso's other reason for accounting for his dark side was because it made him more dependent on God's grace. This is not to say, "let us sin so that grace may abound" (Rom. 6:1). Rather, we're saying that self-awareness of our dark side and of all its secret machinations will highlight to us the need for God's undeserved kindness.

Most of us go about life unaware of our desperate need for God's moment-by- moment mercy. We might become aware of our need for grace when we commit an obvious sin that we already believed to be bad ("I spent too long looking at that beautiful woman," "I didn't entirely disclose the truth to my husband about how much I spent"), but how many of us are in touch with the *constancy* of our need? Jonathan Edwards famously said that we dangle on a mere thread over God's justice like a spider dangles over a flame by a single thread. Do we understand how very thin this thread is?

Being in touch with our dark side makes us feel our desperation. Understanding its slippery nature and how it leaves us with an inner bankruptcy opens our eyes to the fact that it is God's grace alone that upholds us and prevents an army of disasters from besieging us. Our dark side reveals how very close to us is the cliff of impending danger at every moment. For the Christian who desires intimacy with God and a greater capacity to follow Him, this sense of dependency on God's grace is the soul's most important medicine.

So don't shy away from facing your dark side if you want to become more differentiated and resilient. Get in touch with your tendency to overdo bad things and underdo good things, your gullibility in believing untruths, your susceptibility to cultivate unwarranted fears and anxieties, and your vulnerability to the negative influences of others. Don't hide from your quickness to give in to exhaustion when you ought to keep going, or your frequent willingness to succumb to dubious desires, or your inability to maintain a consistently good attitude. Courageously look at your failure to remember important truths and your ineptitude at restraining yourself in the face of overwhelming temptations.

Accounting for all these weaknesses and limitations, without fear or shame, is a gateway to resiliency. The more you face the darkness, the tougher your inner life will become, not because you'll grow hardened and cynical, but because you'll grow more sober-minded. Peter wrote that sober-mindedness is a pre-condition for spiritual action (1 Pet. 1:13), for prayer (1 Pet. 4:7) and for resisting the devil (1 Pet. 5:8), all elements of resilience. It will cause your growth in the kind of wisdom that is productive and fruitful for God's Kingdom, even when enduring trials and hardships. Your darkness, if observed objectively instead of with defensiveness, will actually turn you toward God's grace rather than away from it.

Chapter Eight:
Nurture Your
Re-created Self

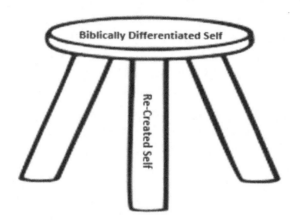

Alfonso, Petr and Jennifer

While Alfonso was lost in thought, Jen silently rehearsed all her regrets and anxieties from the last few days. She found herself sliding back and forth between blame and anger on the one hand, and remorse and trepidation on the other.

Jen would think of one of Petr's poor coping mechanisms, like the way he handled criticism by trying harder to please people, and anger would flare up in her heart. How could he be so stupid?! If Petr wasn't already dead when they found him, she'd kill him herself for all the pain he'd put her through. These past hours of analyzing his private shortcomings with Alfonso had left her feeling betrayed and hurt. How could *she* have been so stupid to put up with all his devious tricks and his lack of integrity? Now her anger flared up at herself.

Then her thoughts would swing suddenly toward remorse when she'd remember that she might very well find her husband dead in a matter of minutes. How could she be angry with Petr when he was in the depths of despair? She couldn't forget some of the negative things she'd said to him lately. One conversation in particular kept floating back to her unbidden. It had been just a couple days ago:

"Jen, I just can't take it anymore. I've got to get out of this unending nightmare," Petr had said for what seemed like the hundredth time that week.

"Honey," Jen had said rather abruptly, in her I'm-done-with-this-conversation tone of voice, "Nothing truly bad has actually happened yet. The board has only been disagreeing with you. Nobody's fired you, or docked your pay, or anything. It's just some negative interactions. Please try to get some perspective."

"But that's almost worse, don't you see?"

"Not really," she'd said with unhidden exasperation.

"It means disaster is about to strike! It means my world is about to collapse all around me. It means my life's basically over, Jen. Don't you get that?"

"Petr," Jen winced at the memory of the tough tone she'd taken with Petr in that moment. Back then, if she'd known he was going to attempt suicide, would she have been so firm? She sighed with regret, wondering if his final significant encounter with her would be this one in which he didn't hear any compassion in her voice.

"Petr. Seriously. Where is God in all this? Where is your confident attitude as a child of God? Doesn't Romans 8 say…"

"Stop quoting Scripture at me Jen. It does no good. So just…."

"Doesn't Romans 8 say," Jen had stubbornly continued, "that you can call God 'Abba' and that His Spirit will 'help you in your weaknesses'? Doesn't Colossians 3:3 say you're 'hidden in Christ'? Hasn't God promised to…"

"Just stop beating me up with the Bible Jen!" Petr's voice was raised now. Jen could tell he was angry with her. "Whenever I try to unburden my heart to you, all you do is throw Scripture at me. I tell you, I've seriously had enough!"

But Jen was mad by this point and knew from long experience that backing down wouldn't help when Petr was like this. "You're right Petr; *I* shouldn't be quoting Scripture at you — *you* should be quoting it to yourself. Why aren't you shoring yourself up by telling these truths to yourself? Just two weeks ago you preached about how we should, 'tell ourselves the truth when we're in a tough situation.' Why aren't you doing it yourself? Weren't you talking about being an 'overcomer' and about being 'seated with Christ in heavenly realms'? Weren't you reminding everyone that 'in all things God works for the good of those who love Him, who have been called according to His purpose'"?

"Jen, Jen, you know that's just what the people want to hear. That's the only reason I say any of that crap; it's all to appease them. That's the only reason any of those people come to church in the first place. They want to get their little weekly pep talk from me. All I am to them is their personal little cheerleader: Go Jimmy go! Go Sally go! And then they get to leave feeling all good and superior about themselves. And you're right," Petr's tone shifted from anger to despair now, "I am just a hypocrite. And when this church crumbles, it … it's going to be all my fault!"

Jen winced again at how she hadn't stopped berating him when Petr had obviously slipped into anguish at that point. She'd gone on and on about how she couldn't believe Petr could be so cynical; cynical about the church members, cynical about his calling, and worst of all, cynical about Scripture. Petr had only held his head in his hands and moaned slowly to himself "gotta get out of this unending nightmare. Gotta get out…"

With a big sigh, Jen wondered to herself for the hundredth time that day if things would be unfolding differently right now if she'd shown more compassion in that conversation…

Nurture the Re-created Self

Petr's interaction with Jennifer is not much different from the inner struggles of many church leaders and pastors at one time or another. Like most, he was going through a season of intense doubt about his calling and about the applicability of God's truth to his own identity.

Perhaps Jen had been too harsh. Or perhaps she was speaking the truth and Petr just couldn't hear it in that moment. Whatever judgment we might wish to give Jennifer for her delivery, we can say in her defense that she was still nobly clinging to the re-created self as a light and a hope in a dark season. And though Petr's doubts are part of the normal struggle common to all believers, and especially to Christian leaders, how might things have been different if he had been nurturing this re-created self instead of spurning it?

We contend that a key part of fostering a biblically differentiated self is to nurture your re-created self. As in the previous chapter, we unfold how to do this with several wise tips.

Tip One: Preach the Truth to Yourself

Our first tip is to preach the truth to yourself. If you're a preacher, you know how to proclaim and admonish others in the truth. Are you doing it to yourself? If you're not a preacher, we'll ask it a different way. Are you telling yourself the truth? More specifically, are you telling yourself the truth about your new, re-created identity in Christ? In other words, are you using truth from Scripture to reprogram your outlook on your identity?

You may be tempted to skip over this part because it seems so basic. If you're a pastor, or you've been in church leadership for a long time, it is quite likely that this concept of learning your new identity in Christ was introduced to you at a very early stage of spiritual development. You were probably taught in those early stages to tell yourself that you were a "child of God" (John 1:12, 1 John 5:1) and not a child of this world any longer. You were likely told that you were "more than a conqueror" (Rom. 8:37), or that, though you had been an "object of wrath" (Rom. 9:22) and "dead in your transgressions and sin" (Eph. 2:1), you'd been graciously "made alive in Christ" (Eph. 2:6) "because of His great love for us" (Eph. 2:4) and now you are a "new creation in Christ" (2 Cor. 5:17). You've covered this territory before. There is no need for a review, you might be thinking.

Or is there? Is there no further frontier in your soul that needs transformation through God's truth? Are there no hidden cracks and fissures in your sense of self that need repair? Were these truths intended only for children and spiritual newcomers? We contend that these truths are applicable throughout the entire Christian journey. What's more, they are applicable in ever deepening ways.

Sufferings tend to challenge our belief in these truths about our identity, no matter how sincerely we once clung to them. Who hasn't questioned the veracity of her own status as a child of God, especially during a time of extreme lack? For example, we know we're supposed to be able to ask God for "anything" and that He "will do it" (John 14:14), but this can be hard to keep believing, even for the most seasoned Christian, when things feel pinched.

Or how about when you endure a difficulty, and all anyone can quote to you is Romans 8:28: "God causes all things to work together for good to those who love God, to those who are called according to His purpose"? This can feel like an annoying, laughable and inapplicable verse when times are tough. The very sound of others citing this text can feel like fingernails on a chalkboard.

We mention all this because we believe that times of trial are times for deepening our application of these truths to our identity, not backing away from them. And yet back away is what we often do, even battle-tested spiritual leaders like pastors. At least, this is what many of us do in secret.

We tend to quote Romans 12:2 mainly to new Christians or to teenagers whose music choices we disapprove of: "And do not be conformed to this world, but be transformed by the renewing of your mind, so that you may prove what the will of God is, that which is good and acceptable and perfect." But what does this passage mean for a seasoned ministry veteran like you? Is there no more transformation for you to experience? Are you already free from conformity to the world in its every form? Do you no longer have ambitions like the world does? Do you no longer struggle with insecurity like the world does? Are you no longer absorbed with yourself like most others?

Following the logic of this passage's syntax (the chapter begins with a "therefore" in verse 1), we know that Paul was connecting this exhortation to the content of the previous 11 chapters. These first 11 chapters expounded on the history of God's merciful dealings with Israel, all leading to the inevitable and profound conclusion that God's righteousness had now appeared "apart from the Law" (Rom. 3:21) through Jesus Christ. Has this reality already transformed your life so much that you can claim total freedom from a worldly outlook on life?

And this passage's standard doesn't seem to equate transformation with being "no longer conformed to the pattern of this world." No, the passage points us to transformation as the capacity to "test and approve God's good, pleasing and perfect will." Do you find God's will so good, pleasing and perfect that you approve of it with all your heart, without reservation, all the time? Or do you have further to go on the journey of approving God's will and finding it pleasurable?

No matter how elementary this practice seems, it is critical that you preach the truth to yourself. Saturate yourself in the truth of Scripture about yourself. The more often, the better. Daily even. Does this mean that your private devotions should resemble the devotions you had when you first committed your life to Christ? Hopefully, your devotions have evolved and deepened. This daily saturation doesn't have to be as elemental as it used to be when you first began learning about your new identity in Christ.

For instance, there are seasons when God will want you to put a pause on reading new Scripture, and He'll call you to meditate on one old truth over and over again. There are other seasons that He'll want you to march along through the entire Bible without pausing even to glance this way or that. But whatever the structure of this daily saturation, continue to immerse your outlook about yourself into the Bible's definition of your re-created self.

This practice of preaching the truth to yourself is a recognition that we are a Gospel-dependent people. In this context, we mean that your emotional maturity, your ability to be a resilient leader, depends on God's grace to you. You access this grace when you cling on by faith to the Bible's truths about yourself. You access deeper grace when you keep clinging on over many years by ever deepening reliance on these truths.

Preaching the truth to yourself will increase your differentiation and thus your resiliency. As you tell yourself what is true, you feed your re-created self on the grace God has already proclaimed to you in the Bible. This is the nourishment your re-created self needs to flourish, to grow strong and to reject fusion with other people.

Tip Two: Suspect Suspicion

Petr fell into cynicism about the applicability of God's truth to his identity. In the moment when faith mattered most, when there was a chance that it would rescue him out of his despair, Petr regarded it with suspicion, as laughable.

But you can avoid the cynicism and despair into which Petr fell by suspecting the suspicion. Suspicion of the truthfulness of the Bible is both historically common and currently fashionable in the Western world. Suspicion has become a litmus test of someone's credibility in many respects in the Western world. Many won't find a speaker or author or preacher to be authentic unless he or she first expresses overwhelming doubt.

But we encourage you to push past your cynicism and choose to look at the Bible's truths about yourself with the wondering eyes of a child. Choose to trust that somehow, in some way or another, God's new identity in Christ applies to you and to your situation. Often, the application is obscure at first, and rapid changes in our society's values can often leave us wondering whether certain truths from Scripture no longer apply. It seems at times as if society has outpaced Scripture in truth. But we must push through to the point of seeing where God's truths about our identity apply, in spite of the suspicion.

This will help you differentiate and become more resilient because it will re-introduce hope into your soul. An unintended consequence of the fashionableness of suspicion is that it has robbed many of hope. But hope is essential for resilience. It is also necessary for differentiation. People often become fused with others and over-identify with them when they already live in a vacuum of hope. They can't find hope in their own souls, so they seek it from the soul of another. Without hope in your own heart, it feels necessary to cling to others and to look to them for it. But when we feel a substantial amount of hope, our soul feels strong enough to journey on without clinging to others.

So suspect this fashionable tendency to be suspicious. Choose hope instead.

Tip Three: Beware of Scarcity

One crucial Scriptural truth that merits highlighting is the idea that in Christ we have all we truly need. Paul rebuked the Corinthians' inappropriate over-identification with human leaders (1 Cor. 1:12) by telling them that identification with Christ was more than sufficient for them. He told them that Christ, not any human leader, was the "power of God and the wisdom of God" (1 Cor. 1:24), that He was their "righteousness and sanctification and redemption" (1 Cor. 1:30).

Many of us fuse with others because we have an internal sense of emptiness. We grasp at the nearest people who are the most attractive, either physically or emotionally, and we look for something in them to fill that sense of emptiness. We're not even referring to romantic interest in others—we do this even in our search for innocent friendships.

But we must be wary of this sense of emptiness and scarcity. It is generally a route to fusion with others.

The antidote is to reject this sense of scarcity and to see our fullness in Christ. As you tell yourself the truth about your re-created self, combine it with truth about the total adequacy of Christ. Jesus is your bread of life (John 6:35 and vs. 48). He is your living water (John 7:38-39), your light (John 9:5), your good shepherd (John 10:11), your resurrection and life (John 11:25), and your true vine (John 15:5) from which flows all you need to bear fruit for Him.

To help you reject scarcity and embrace Christ's fullness, meditate on what His fullness means for you. For instance, because He is your true vine, you may "ask whatever we wish, and it will be done for" you (John 15:8). Or because Jesus is your bread of life, you know that if you come to Him you will not become spiritually hungry and if you believe in Him, you will not be spiritually thirsty (John 6:35). Scripture is brimming with truths about how our identity as His children (John 1:12) with special access to Him leaves us spiritually full because of the adequacy of Christ.

Think of how John describes our status as sons and daughters of God. The NIV explains it this way: "See what great love the Father has lavished on us, that we should be called children of God!" (1 John 3:1). *Great* love. *Lavish* love. These words do not depict a miserly God who has reluctantly adopted us and barely tolerates us. They speak of a God who is eager to make us His children. Our very status as adopted children is an expression of this lavish love of God.

Or consider Paul's language about our new identity in Christ: "*In love* He predestined us for adoption..." (Eph. 1:4-5). In other words, God adopted us with a loving attitude and He decided to do it even before meeting us! This adoption happened, "in accordance with His pleasure and will" (vs. 5). In other words, God *wanted* to adopt us and He took pleasure in the adoption. It says later in verse 8 that He "lavished" His grace on us, and that He did it "with all wisdom and understanding." Adopting us was a smart thing for God to do. He did it "according to His good pleasure" (vs. 9). Again, God liked this adoption process. And He likes us. We please Him simply by being His children.

It is important that you drill down into this idea that your identity in Christ is an expression of God's abundance rather a sign of scarcity. The more you reject the scarcity mindset and embrace your fullness in Christ, the less tempted you will be to over-identify with others. This in turn will allow you to differentiate more fully and become more resilient.

Chapter Nine:
Nurture Your Self-in-Relation with the Creator and the Created

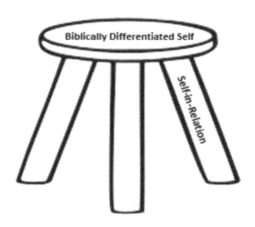

Alfonso, Petr and Jennifer

Jennifer pulled out of her daze and began to recognize the Interstate landmarks. Their turnoff was fast approaching. A well-lit sign announcing the nearby Indianapolis Motor Speedway came into view.

"Almost there…" she barely whispered.

"Mm," was all Alfonso could say in reply.

"Al, I know I've said this like a hundred times already, but I really don't think I can handle this. I mean, what if…"

"Jen," Alfonso remembered to be a little more pastoral, "I think we should pray."

"You're right," she said dully. Right now she couldn't force that confident tone in prayer she normally assumed as the senior pastor's wife when she was in front of the congregation. In fact, she wasn't sure she had it in her to pray at all right now. At the moment all she could think of was how little help prayer seemed to have been up to this point. Why hadn't God heard all their previous cries for help?

But Alfonso launched right in: "God, we know you're here with us. We don't understand why all this has happened this way so far. It doesn't make sense. But things don't have to make sense for us to follow You. You are a mysterious and sovereign God. I pray that whatever happens, God, that You'd enable Jennifer and me to be faithful to You. Help us with … with whatever we discover …"

Jennifer felt something inside her rise up with desperation. She interrupted: "And God, please rescue Petr. Please pluck him out of this trouble. Remind him of Your goodness, even though he can't see it right now. I know he's tasted and seen that You're good. It's been a long time since he remembered it, but I know he's tasted it in the past. Please intervene … God … please God …" Jen broke out in new sobs.

Alfonso reached over to lay a hand on Jennifer's shoulder and continued: "And God, we pray that even right now you'd begin to heal all those ways Petr got himself into trouble. All the ways he used people, and all the ways he let people use him, please begin healing and correcting him right now. Please touch him and start healing how he neglected his true self. Show him a way out of this mess. He kept calling for a way out of his nightmare. Please show him the way out by healing his relationships with other people and with You. God, we 'don't know what do to, but our eyes are on you!' Please God. In Jesus' mighty and all-powerful name, Amen."

Both were quiet for a long time after they prayed. Finally, as her tears died down, Jen spoke up. "Al? Do you really think God can heal Petr from all that stuff we were talking about? Do you actually believe there's hope for him? I mean, all that darkness in his heart runs so deep."

"Jen, what I know is that God can heal anybody, of anything. I don't know if Petr will be willing, but I know God has enough power and enough love. I know God can show him how to order his relationships in a redemptive way. Jen, all I can do in a time like this is cling to God."

"Yep," she said, not fully convinced. "I'm trying to do the same."

"Here's the off ramp Jen..."

Nurture Your Self-in-Relation with the Creator and the Created

We made the argument back in Chapter Four that differentiation (and thus resiliency) is all about relationships, both with God and with others. This chapter explores the final leg of the stool of a biblically differentiated self: Our self-in-relation with God and with others.

With the Creator

In Chapter Four we argued that the more authentic and non-exploitative your relationship with God can be, the more you will have an inner capacity to have differentiated relationships with others, relationships in which you treasure humans for their own sake, in imitation of Jesus' example and in response to His command to love as He loved (John 13:34, 15:12).

But how do you cultivate an authentic, non-exploitative relationship with the Eternal God?

At this point, we could turn this into a chapter all about the spiritual disciplines, or all about how to practice the "means of grace," like prayer, Scripture study, tithing, church fellowship, and so on. These are certainly helpful and even necessary for connecting with God. But even these can turn into opportunities to exploit God if approached with the wrong attitude. How many of us have turned prayer, for instance, into a means of securing things from God as if He were no more than the Heavenly Vending Machine?

Instead, our advice in this chapter targets our inner postures toward God. Spiritual disciplines, while good and necessary, can leave us thinking that we are in the driver's seat of differentiation. In reality, differentiation is work that *God* sovereignly does in us. So, keep practicing spiritual disciplines in partnership with Him, but do so with the following postures of openness to what God wants to do in you.

Tip One: Make Peace with the Mysteriousness of God

One of the most foundational elements of cultivating an authentic and non-exploitative relationship with God is to make peace with the mysteriousness of God.

American Christianity, especially in the last 75 years, is bloated with efforts to simplify and explain away God's mysteriousness to a public that has come to expect spiritual fast food. Well-meaning pastors, Christian radio and television personalities and evangelists have spent decades selling a more easily understood and paradox-free God. When Christian leaders have wondered how to captivate hearts and minds in an increasingly secular culture, many have responded by thinking, "This growing secularism is just a simple packaging and PR problem. Let's do what all successful businesses do and present a more user-friendly God. Problem solved!" So, we've pushed the inconvenient and more puzzling elements of Christian doctrine to the side. And now the church is full of generations of Christians who won't have their God any other way than the well marketed, comfortable and easy-to-consume McGod.

This effort isn't without precedent. Throughout most of the history of the church, some Christian leaders and teachers have chosen to minimize certain parts of Christian doctrine because they were just too confusing. For instance, for centuries many streams in Western Christianity have declared that the Holy Spirit, the Third Person of the Trinity, was inactive because it was too confusing to attempt to elaborate on His mysterious nature or on His mysterious activity among and inside God's people. But can we really have a Christianity without the active participation of one of the Members of the Godhead? Fortunately, wiser heads have prevailed in more recent decades on this issue.

An authentic relationship with Him must come to terms with His mysteriousness as He is presented in Scripture, rather than with the tidy, clearly explainable God that the American church has re-presented to the culture.

Every one of the patriarchs, every one of the prophets, every one of the good judges or kings or queens who sought to follow God, every one the disciples, wrestled mightily with a God they could not understand, a God who defied all explanations, a God who left them all troubled and wondering.

Think through each character you know in Scripture. Did any of them know an easy-to-understand God? Did Abraham when he was called to sacrifice Isaac? Did Joseph when he languished year after year in prison? Did Moses when he saw his people wander in circles for forty years?

Or what about the Prophet Elijah when he witnessed wicked leadership go without punishment for decades, despite his powerful miracles? Did Ezekiel when God told him He would soon take away his wife? Did any of the disciples anticipate Jesus' death and resurrection as the long awaited messianic solution? Did they comprehend it and embrace it when it happened before their very eyes?

Each of these had to make peace with a God who was too big to comprehend; whose ways were too unsearchable, whose strategies were too inscrutable for mortal minds. We must likewise make peace with this mysterious God if we hope to cultivate an authentic relationship with Him.

Now, you should not use the "mysteriousness of God" as an excuse for theological laziness. Rather, keep digging vigorously into the mysteries of God with all your heart and all your mind, because God loves the seeker. You also should not do what Christian leaders have done for centuries: use the mysteriousness of God to dismiss important questions by skeptics, new believers and children. Countless numbers of people have been chased away from even beginning to believe by Christian leaders who, insecure in their own faith, have rebuked inquirers with, "How dare you question! God is just mysterious. You've just got to have faith!" Christian leaders should encourage spiritual curiosity in all its forms, rather than shut down probing minds.

God's mysteriousness also does not mean that all the truths He has revealed are overly complex. God has communicated some of His mysteries to us in simple ways, with unambiguous language, and He wants us to understand those. And He wants you, as a Christian leader, to work hard at making them understandable to people at every level, from small children to the most educated adults.

———

Nor does it not mean that He is comprehensible only to the intellectually sophisticated. On the contrary, God "makes foolish the wisdom of this world" (1 Cor. 1:20), a reference by Paul to the educated elite of his day, "the scribe ... the debater ..." God has always delighted in revealing Himself to children, to the "least of these" (Matt. 25:40-45), to those who are not able to use sharp mental acumen to apprehend Him. He has always delighted in confounding the worldly wise.

But we do need to surrender to God's essential mysteriousness. For you personally, if you want to have an authentic, non-exploitative relationship with God, you need to accept the truth that God is deeply mysterious and that His ways are mysterious. A mysterious God is an uncontrollable God. A mysterious God is a God we cannot manipulate. A mysterious God defies exploitation.

When Job suffered so terribly he demanded some sort of explanation of the suffering from God. Why should he, a righteous man, endure the sufferings meant for the wicked? God, in His mysteriousness, eventually did show up, but not with an explanation. Instead, God revealed His power. Job's final conclusion, after this revelation of God's mysterious power, was:

I know You can do all things, and that
no purpose of Yours can be thwarted …
Therefore I have declared that which I did
not understand, things too wonderful for
me, which I did not know … I have heard
of you by the hearing of the ear; But now
my eye sees You; Therefore I retract, and I
repent in dust and ashes (Job 41:2-6).

Job finally reached a level of peace in the midst
of his sufferings when he stopped fighting the
mysteriousness of God.

Petr's God had been reduced down to
something he could exploit for his own sense of
success in ministry. His was not the mysterious
God. Who is your God?

Tip Two: Delight in the Delightfulness of God

God's mysteriousness can actually
become a thrill if you simultaneously learn to
delight in His delightfulness.

Something that King David knew,
something that King Saul never seemed to
discover, was that wrapped up in God's
mysteriousness was an essentially delightful
God. David exhorted worshipers to "taste and
see that the Lord is good" (Ps. 34:8) because he

knew that, no matter how inscrutable God's ways were, at His core He was good and loving. David was so convinced of the fundamental goodness of God that he wrote, "because your loving-kindness is better than life, my lips will praise you. So I will bless you as long as I live; I will lift up my hands in Your name. My soul is satisfied as with marrow and fatness, and my mouth offers praises with joyful lips" (Ps. 63:3-5). David experienced an enjoyment of God that flowed from a deep certainty that God's loving-kindness was superior to and bigger than life itself.

In the same way, Christians are called into an enjoyment of God based on His essential goodness. If we believe that God at His core is very good, then the possibility exists for us to enjoy Him. Christians can experience delight because they know that God is delightfully good.

It nurtures an authentic relationship with God when we delight in His delightfulness. This is because it assumes the very best about His character. It posits Him in the best light possible and takes as trustworthy Scripture's revelations that, whatever else God might be, however unpredictable and fearsome, He is good.

We cannot truly delight in another person if we are suspicious of his motives, nitpicky of his behavior, and wary of his next move, as if at his core he were a slippery character. When you choose to see the very best in a person, a new world opens up in your capacity to enjoy him. Even his surprises and unexpected moves turn into an adventure.

It is the same way with God. When your unmovable and bedrock conviction about Him is that He is good, whatever else He may be, then even His surprising moves can bring the thrill of a roller coaster. If you are one of those people who enjoys a good roller coaster, probably one of the things you like about them is the unexpected zig just when you thought it was going to zag. You were anticipating a jolt to the right, but instead you got a jolt to the left and then downward. Rather than making you feel as if your world were being torn apart and your equilibrium irreparably broken, a roller coaster is exciting in part because you know, despite its jarring shocks, that it will bring you back safely. This leaves you free simply to enjoy the ride.

In this way, God's delightfulness works in tandem with His mysteriousness. God's mysteriousness might rough you up quite a bit, giving you unwelcome zigs when you were expecting zags. But if you believe God is good before He is anything else, then even the wild careening of life's ups and downs can be a kind of secret thrill instead of a traumatizing terror. In fact, God's kindnesses can become all the more enjoyable because of their unpredictability.

God has a way of startling us with unforeseen and unplanned gifts and mercies. But we are generally blind to His surprising intrusions of kindness into our lives unless we are also open to His mysteriousness. When we are open to and accepting of God's mysteriousness, we become more ready to recognize and enjoy the unanticipated ways in which He shows up. So, mysteriousness actually enhances the enjoyment of God's goodness, because it makes us more ready to delight in the inherent delightfulness of this wild and uncontrollable God.

Seeing God as good in this way, in conjunction with embracing His mysteriousness, removes our ability to exploit Him. Only an untrustworthy God needs to be manipulated by our rituals, our works-righteousness, and our bargaining prayers. But a trustworthy God, a good God, a delightful God, can simply be surrendered to and enjoyed.

Tip Three: Embrace the Sovereignty of God

This mysterious and delightful God is also the master of the vast and unsearchable universe. He is Creator and Upholder of all things, including your very life.

By Him all things were created, both in the heavens and on earth, visible and invisible, whether thrones or dominions or rulers or authorities – all things have been created through Him and for Him. He is before all things, and in Him all things hold together (Col. 1:16-17).

All things happen, all events unfold, all history progresses, and all solar systems spin only as a result of His express command. Nothing happens outside His command. Only God has an exhaustive and precise catalogue in His mind of all that exists, has existed and ever will exist. He is intimately familiar with the smallest sub-atomic activities and with the twirlings of the grandest galaxy. And it all moves exactly according to His desire.

The very breath you draw at this moment is a loan from God, an expression of His inscrutable wish to extend life to you. The same is true of your next breath, and the next. God arranges all the days of your life as well as all that has led up to your life and to this exact moment, in all its nearly infinite detail. He could tell you about each and every one of your heartbeats because each and every one occurred only because of His conscious volition. He could tell you about each and every thought and feeling you've ever experienced every minute of all your days, since before your birth, because you've not escaped His notice for even a moment.

This is the fearsome Sovereign to whom you owe your very life. It is because of Him that you live at this moment. Your very existence hangs on the mere thread of His good pleasure, and for no other reason.

This is the sovereign being who controls the most distant cluster of stars and who has determined their exact numbers of days. It is because of Him that the universe has been stretched out to its current incomprehensible breadth and crowded with uncountable heavenly bodies.

It is by embracing this *sovereign* God that you will make progress in your differentiation and resiliency. Many Christians feel compelled to fuse with other people and with circumstances and with idols because their view of God's authority and sovereignty is so small.

If you view God in some way to not be in charge of a part of your life, then that is a part of your life you will have no choice but to fret over. In other words, if God is not sovereign over something, then it is vain to entrust that something to His care and power. This opens the door to be anxious about something, which in turn opens the next door to fuse with the people and circumstances and idols that appear to offer relief from that anxiety.

For instance, if you view God as not having the authority and power to take care of your marriage, then the only means available to you to make it a good marriage is to rely on yourself and your spouse. This means that only the two of you have all the wisdom, all the insight, all the energy, all the resources necessary to make it a good marriage. This means that you will likely put a lot of pressure on yourself. But even more likely than that, it means that you will put an enormous amount of pressure on your spouse. He or she has to be the perfect spouse. It will become *their* responsibility to be perfectly dutiful, a great listener, the most compassionate and understanding, the most thoughtful, and the best anticipator of your needs. In the absence of a God who is sovereign over your marriage, you will fuse yourself to this image of a perfect spouse.

Does this sound like a set of expectations that will make for a successful marriage?

But a sovereign God frees you from needing to fuse yourself to people and circumstances and idols. When others fail you and let you down, it is OK because your welfare was never in their hands to begin with. When circumstances disappoint you, it is OK because your welfare never relied on those circumstances to begin with. It all depends on an all-powerful God, a God who is able to accomplish His will in your life, from beginning to end.

Furthermore, a sovereign God cannot be manipulated. This works in the same way that making peace with God's mysteriousness defies manipulation. You cannot control a sovereign God or anticipate His next move. You can only respond in awe and humility.

This is how you should regard God if you hope to cultivate an authentic versus an exploitative relationship with Him.

Thus, to make progress in differentiation and resiliency, it is critical that you enlarge your view of God's sovereignty. We will leave it to other, better written books to tackle the ancient theological controversy of God's sovereignty versus human free will. But for the sake of your personal development, for your personal advancement in peace and differentiation, embrace God's sovereignty.

Tip Four: Practice Submission and Surrender

If God is sovereign, then you owe Him your allegiance. The surest way of avoiding an exploitative relationship with God is to practice submission and surrender to His revealed will. Nothing better demonstrates an authentic relationship with God than a willingness to submit. Conversely, nothing more accurately exposes your exploitative relationship with Him than your unwillingness to submit and surrender to Him.

Jesus tackled this issue poignantly when He exalted His disciples to the status of "friends" (John 15:14-15). He explained to them "You are my friends if you do what I command you." According to Jesus, obedience is the mark of friendship with God. Far from being a sign of servility, Jesus regarded obedience to be a sign of intimacy with Him. A servant or slave "does not know what his master is doing." Thus, the obedience of a servant comes from blindness and a lack of intimacy. But in Jesus' mind, the obedience of a friend comes from intimately knowing the One whom they obey.

But this kind intimate knowing is quite different from the sort more often encouraged in Western Christianity. Western Christians are far more likely to hear about and embrace a version of intimacy with God that is in reality just over-familiarity. Western Christians hear many pleas to draw close to God and to experience Him in intimate knowing. This is often communicated by using the metaphor of two human lovers who enjoy equal status.

This metaphor has some biblical basis, particularly in the Song of Solomon. But unfortunately, as well meaning as the promoters of this metaphor may be, its overuse and misapplication has unintentionally introduced Western Christians to a view of intimacy with God in which there does not need to be respect, fear or adoration. In this view, there does not need to be a sense of the holiness and sacredness of God, or of His exalted status as superior to us.

It is understandable that Western Christians would like this alternative view of intimacy. We've always loved to democratize everything and everyone, and we tend to feel a visceral sense of injustice if anyone, including God, gets to be superior. But the unintended consequence of this is that we've become like the rich child who gets spoiled from over-familiarity with her nanny.

Imagine the little brat who talks back to her nanny. The nanny's employers have told her that she can't discipline her charge so she is helpless in the face of disrespect. With impunity the child barks out orders to the nanny using her first name and in a demanding tone of voice. She's sassy and throws temper tantrums when she fears that she won't get her way. In one way, this looks a little like intimacy because the two are on a first name basis in their relationship and because they appear to behave as equals, with the child just as powerful as, if not more than, the nanny. But this "intimacy" is really just over-familiarity. It is just another occasion for one person to exploit another.

Lots of other relationships appear intimate but are actually exploitative. Parasites surely feel intimate with their hosts, pressed up against them and burrowing into their skin or intestinal wall like they do. Pedophiles often report feeling very "intimate" with the children they abuse because of the nature of the physical contact between them. But in reality, the pedophile is merely exploiting the child for his own satisfaction and entirely at the child's expense.

Practicing submission and surrender to God prevents you from this masquerade of intimacy in which you use Him as a mere psychological crutch. Lots of Christians will testify to their deep intimacy with God because of all the powerful feelings they experience in worship or prayer. But surrender to His will is the true test of whether or not you are God's "friend" as He defines the word.

Fused, over-identifying relationships with people, circumstances and idols, the kind that drag you down and prevent your resiliency, result from an exploitative relationship with God. But you can nurture an authentic, non-exploitative relationship with God by making peace with His mysteriousness, delighting in His delightfulness, embracing His sovereignty, and practicing submission and surrender to His revealed will.

With the Created

As your relationship with God increases in its authenticity, there is ever-greater hope that you will be able to have more differentiated relationships with people, which in turn leads to greater resiliency.

Tip One: Treasure People for Their Sake

The first and most critical piece of advice for nurturing the self-in-relation with the created is to treasure people for their own sake, rather than for their perceived benefits to you.

Treasuring people for their sake begins by disavowing all the ways, both overt and subtle, that we exploit others. We've already explained in previous chapters how we fall into the rut, often unintentionally, of valuing people because we can benefit from them in some way.

The most extreme examples of exploitative relationships are slave and master relationships or relationships in which an adult takes sexual advantage of a minor or of a vulnerable adult. But many of our relationships exploit others in much more subtle ways. For instance, if you manage other people at your work or place of ministry, it is easy to slip into seeing these people as merely tools to accomplish your goals and make you look good. Their successes and failures are only important in so far as they demonstrate your successes or failures.

329

But it gets even subtler than this. For example, we often raise our children imagining them to be extensions of us. Their successes and failures reflect ours, which increase our need to manage the image of the whole family. Spouses, ironically, are often the biggest targets of our exploitative impulses. We use them because they can help us get through life better than we can do on our own. Does your spouse have much value to you beyond what he or she can do for you?

As you rid yourself of your exploitative view of people, you must replace it with a God's-eye view of people. At its most basic level, this means applying one's new identity in Christ to other people and choosing to value them because of the delight God takes in them. All the truths we discussed in previous chapters about your created and re-created self are applicable to other people. The more we can look at people through this lens the more valuable they will appear to us for their own sake rather than for our sake.

A good exercise is to meditate on specific individuals, especially those for whom it is a struggle to see in a non-exploitive way, by prayerfully imagining all the ways that their new identity in Christ benefits them. Think through all the ways those Scripture passages mentioned in previous chapters apply to them. Try to do this in as detailed a way as possible. Pause and pray through these passages for those individuals.

As you do this, ask for God's Spirit to enlighten them about these truths so that they might enjoy their full benefit. Paul did this in his prayers for the Ephesians (Eph. 1:15-23, 3:14-19) and the Philippians (Phil. 1:3-11). Doing this will help you gain a God's-eye view of these other people.

In addition to meditating and praying about others' re-created selves, meditate and pray about their created selves. Give thanks for each and every quality and characteristic of another person of which you are aware. Get as detailed as you possibly can. Ask God to bless all these aspects of their created selves.

While meditating this way, ask yourself this question: "Would I value this person if I gained no benefit from him whatsoever?" Imagine this person as offering no benefit to you of any kind. Imagine him apart from any perceived contributions he can make to you or to others. Imagine his value before God, simply for existing. Would he still be valuable if he weren't your employee? Your child? Your spouse? Would she still be valuable if she weren't your co-worker with a skill you need to make use of for your own success? What if he is a volunteer on whom you depend to run the children's ministry at your church?

As you do this, you will notice the Holy Spirit enlarge your heart for other people. This exercise will re-train the way you think about other people. As your brain gets re-trained with truth from Scripture, your heart will inevitably follow suit. It will become harder and harder to exploit others, even in your thoughts, as you learn to treasure people for their own sake.

Treasuring others for their own sake will enable you to better differentiate from them and increase your resiliency. You won't be tempted to latch on to, fuse, or over-identify with a person you see as valuable for his own sake. This is because you will know deep down that they do not exist for your sake. Their gifts and contributions may not be for your benefit.

It is also helpful because your conscience will be enlivened by treasuring others. It will scream out at you in protest to reprimand you if you fall into exploitative attitudes. You will be more able to clearly recognize your exploitative impulses to fuse. And if you can recognize them you will be able to avoid them.

But best of all, imagine how treasuring others for their sake will please the heart of Jesus. He is so fond of those people with whom you share relationships. They are so valuable to Him and His heart is so tender toward them.

Remember how, when Jesus restored Peter to ministry (John 21:15-20), He expressed such concern that Peter feed His sheep (verses 15-17). Jesus calls all Christian leaders to feed His sheep, all because He treasures them so dearly. The more you and I treasure them for their own sake, the closer we are to the heart of Jesus.

Tip Two: Hold On to Yourself

Our second tip is to hold on to yourself in relationships so that you can avoid the danger of fusion in all its forms. This means holding on tightly to your created self and your re-created self *while* in relationship with others, *as* you interact with them.

This involves what we wrote about a couple of chapters ago—celebrating and asserting your created self. This also involves what we wrote about in the last chapter, preaching the truth to yourself. But in this chapter we add a key element: you need to learn how to hold on to yourself not just in the abstract but during the back and forth interactions of a relationship.

Many people avoid asserting their convictions or celebrating their interests in relationships because they fear it will make others see them as unusual. They fear it will rock the boat and alienate others. It feels especially risky if you are trying to get to know people for the first time, or if you are trying to learn the unspoken rules of a community that is new to you.

Sometimes it is wise, especially at first, to keep your convictions, your enjoyments, your interests and your beliefs about your new identity in Christ to yourself. This is especially true as you discover how new relationships and new communities talk about these things. But consider where a relationship goes if one party never unveils her true self. Rather, consider where a relationship does *not* go. The relationship does not become authentic. It cannot go deep. This is not necessarily because the person withholding her convictions, interests and beliefs is consciously deceptive. It is because she never allows herself to be truly known by the other. She never permits any insight past her superficial façade.

Now take it a step further. Consider what happens when two people do attempt to go deep with each other but one member of the duo does not hold on to himself. This is when the relationship is in the greatest danger of fusion or over-identifying with one another. The thing that holds the two parties together will be each one's hopes and expectations in the other to offer friendship, love and commitment. But the hopes and expectations are based on a false presentation.

So, when one party begins to fuse to the other, as inevitably happens, he has become fused to a deception. Such a foundation will not weather future storms and the undifferentiated, fused individuals will be dragged down with those storms.

Fusion threatens in any sort of relationship, both our intimate, pleasurable ones, and our unpleasant ones. Fusion threatens our intimate relationships because we can easily hand the control of our sense of self over to those we love. This is common for us because we tend to trust of our loved ones so much. In our trust, we imagine they are safe enough to have authority over our sense of self. Trust, while generally a positive element of an intimate relationship, makes it more likely that we'll hand over that control. This does not mean we should avoid trust. It just means that when we trust we need to be all the more aware of our vulnerability to fusion.

Our unpleasant relationships also hold the danger of fusion, but for a different reason. We tend to be hyper-vigilant with unpleasant people, and usually rightly so. They pose some sort of risk to us. But the very same hyper-vigilant attitude we use to protect ourselves can tend to overly inflate the threat in our own eyes. This other person feels bigger, stronger, wilier than I am, whether or not he actually is. This perception causes me to believe that he has the power to wrench from me my very sense of identity against my will. The unpleasant person then consumes more of my attention and emotion than is warranted by reality, and I become fused again, but this time through fear.

The solution is a kind of right-sized vigilance that neither lets down our guard for everybody and everything nor does it erect the emotional equivalent of triple layered barbed-wire fences. Right-sized vigilance means having boundaries with other people that are appropriate to the relationship and situation. Good boundaries do not mean being rude or off-putting. If you are a professional minister, rudeness just isn't one of your options.

What does it mean to have appropriate boundaries? Good boundaries mainly involve holding on to yourself resolutely. This begins with celebrating yourself, thanking God for yourself, and asserting yourself, as already described. It also means holding on to your convictions and values. It means refusing to surrender them just for the sake of a false peace. It means holding on to your needs and preferences, interests and attractions, as we described earlier.

Moreover, it means holding on to your space and pace. By this we mean you don't need to let a compulsive hurry-er bully you into rushing faster than you know is good for you. Nor do you need to let a slow poke make you feel guilty for your greater capacity to get more done in a day.

Or, if you're an introvert, don't let extroverts make you feel guilty because you don't work the room with the same self-assurance. If you're an extrovert don't let introverts provoke your jealousy because they appear to have more margin in their lives. Whatever way God has made you hold on to yourself.

Remember our discussion of the Incarnation in Chapter Five? Jesus was able to lay His life down because He held on to His true self.

In addition to consciously holding on to yourself, good boundaries are a conscious refusal to be swallowed up by another. This means denying others the right to pillage your celebration of what God has done in you. Establish good boundaries with people so you can continue to celebrate yourself free from invasion and violation.

How exactly does this work? A loved one thinks it's funny to sarcastically tear down some character trait of yours. You know this is a trait in which God delights. An appropriate boundary is to politely but firmly request that he stop the cruel remarks. When that fails, you politely but firmly remove yourself from situations in which your loved one feels free to crack his disparaging jokes.

A member of the church board likes to throw his weight around to get you, the mere ministry hireling, to do what he wants. You politely but firmly clarify what is his responsibility as a board member and what yours is as a church employee. You value his input but by himself he is not your employer.

Your spouse thinks it's your responsibility to make him happy. He expects you to carry his emotional burdens for him. You politely but firmly remind him that he needs to carry his own emotional load. If he doesn't respectfully respond, you gently but still resolutely withdraw the emotional support to which he has come to feel entitled. "But that might devastate our marriage!" you protest. What is being devastated is the false foundation of fusion. This is the only route to resurrecting your marriage and re-building it on a better foundation.

Whenever we sense that someone wants something from us, something that he or she ought to be getting from God, we must politely but firmly set up clear boundaries. People want to use and even abuse us for some sort of satisfaction or reward, of which God alone is the dispenser. We need to partner with God to erect boundaries that keep turning people back to Him for their needs to be met.

Sometimes these boundaries are spoken out loud: "No, you can't invade my privacy that way." Sometimes they are internal and don't need to be spoken out loud: "I refuse to let him decide if I feel good about myself today." These internal boundaries are usually the most important ones and generally take up more of our time and energy than the external ones. The internal ones usually must precede the external ones. This is true for both intimate relationships and unpleasant ones.

A part of the reason we must hold on to ourselves is the parasitic nature of human sinfulness. Humanity remains, until Christ returns to consummate His Kingdom, enslaved to its sinful nature. This means that people, even those in Christ, have a parasitic element in their hearts that seeks to draw life from others inappropriately instead of drawing it from God. Most people do this unknowingly, and would not be able to detect the impulse in themselves even if they tried. But it is there, nonetheless.

This sounds like we're saying the opposite of what we wrote for the previous section, "Treasure people for their own sake." But it actually isn't. When we treasure people for their own sake, we choose to look at them as God does, through the lens of Christ and His finished work on behalf of humanity. This involves seeing both the good and the ugly in other people.

Frequently, people hesitate to hold on to themselves when in relationships because they believe it is unloving not to satisfy this parasitic element in other people. They worry they are betraying Christ's command to love people self-sacrificially like He loved. "How could it be self-sacrificing to hold on to oneself?" they wonder. But the opposite is actually true. The most loving way to handle parasitic behavior is *not* to appease others' desire for something from you that only God can give. Every time you reward them for looking to you instead of to God to meet their needs, you reinforce their idolatry and set them up for the ultimate failure of neglecting the worship due to God.

There is passive parasitic behavior and aggressive parasitic behavior. The passive parasitic behavior seeks to draw life from us in an indirect way, often through a person's own willful depression, learned helplessness, or a victim mentality and various other forms of quiet manipulation. Someone you're counseling says to you,

> *I guess I'll just go home by myself and be all alone tonight again (big sigh). It's just more loneliness for me. I guess it's just more of me singing my old song "Hello Darkness, My Old Friend" (another big sigh). Story of my life. Oh well.*

This counselee's goal is to get want he wants from you by guilting you into willingly surrendering your inner resources. He wants you to chase him down and offer him all your inner emotional strength that he refuses to muster directly from God. It is a trap for both you and for him.

The goal of those with aggressive parasitic tendencies is the same but they do it through more obviously controlling behaviors like rage, anger, threats and raising their voices. People with this approach try to get what they want out of you by overpowering you: "You're going to change direction on your policy or else!" a parishioner yells at you. He wants to badger or bully you into submission because he needs you to change for him to be happy.

Both the passive and aggressive expressions of the parasitic tendencies require boundaries to avoid fusion and make the relationship comply with God's right order.

Appropriate boundaries evolve over time depending on how the relationship evolves. In this way, good boundaries are like a cast on a broken limb, which protects and sets things in place until the limb is healed and strong. Boundaries protect and set things in place until you are strong enough for relationships with people, all of whom have natural traces of parasitism. You need to be strong enough if you hope to effectively avoid fusion. So, sometimes a relationship must begin with thicker and stronger boundaries. But as you and the other person grow in your levels of differentiation, you can afford to adapt the boundaries according to the reduced risks of fusion.

Even as the boundaries evolve you must always hold on to yourself in the relationship. Until Christ returns, the danger always exists of becoming inappropriately fused to another person, no matter how mature you both may be. So, the right-sized vigilance is always necessary, and holding on to yourself is always necessary. Since healthy relationships will always build up and not tear down the real you — the you God created you to be — you must be vigilant to protect the real you from those relationships that can parasitically drain you. You know you have a well differentiated relationship that is healthy and reflective of God's order when it encourages you to become more of the real you and not less.

Tip Three: Practice Stillness in Threat

Like in any war for survival, sometimes boundaries fail. Your best efforts to set limits on the parasitic tendencies of others can crumble. Your firm verbal clarifications can go unheeded.

Your efforts to create healthy distance fall apart. To prepare for this inevitability you need to learn how to be inwardly still in the face every sort of relational threat.

If you would grow in differentiation and resilience then it is critical for you to practice inner stillness in the face of threat. This means assuring yourself of God's truth about you and about Him in the midst of relational danger so that you can remain calm. When you sense those with parasitic tendencies extending their clutching tentacles toward you to suck out your life, you need to practice stillness. When you sense loved ones inappropriately grasping for your inner resources, you need to practice stillness. When you sense emotional bullies expanding in your direction like ominous, dark thunderclouds, you need to practice stillness. When you sense any anxiety of any amount rise up in association with any relationship of any kind, you need to practice stillness.

Most of us, when our boundaries have been violated, automatically go into fight or flight mode. We tend either to lash back or we seek to escape. But Jesus had a wonderful practice of staying still in the face of threat. When Pharisees accused Him of wrongdoing, He didn't react with equal virulence. He calmly but firmly rebuked them. When He faced arrest, accusations from the High Priest and from Pilot, and when He faced the cross, He was able to stay calm. His only recorded instance of apparently wild violence was when He overturned the money lending tables in the Temple (Matt. 21:12, Mark 11:15, John 2:15). But this was not an unforeseen explosion of rage over an unexpected insult; it was a pre-planned gesture in fulfillment of prophecy.

The Psalmist describes the secret ingredients of remaining inwardly still in the face of threat in Psalms 37 and 46.

In Psalm 37, he exhorts his readers to, "Be still before the Lord and wait patiently for Him; do not fret when people succeed in their ways, when they carry out their wicked schemes" (vs. 7). He reveals the secret to this stillness when he counsels the readers to meditate on the inevitable end of the wicked: "for like the grass they will soon wither, like the green plants they will soon die away" (vs. 2). He promises vindication for those who quietly commit their way to the Lord and trust Him (vs. 6).

When you face various relational threats, of whatever kind, you can practice inward stillness by comforting yourself with similar truths. Your enemy will inevitably falter, be reduced in influence or outright disappear. Even if this doesn't happen fully until Jesus' return, your enemy's failure is inevitable and certain. As difficult as this current trial is you can react with calm by committing your way to the Lord and trusting in God's future vindication of your cause. The vindication may not happen until we see Jesus face-to-face. But it will happen.

Jesus quoted from this Psalm when He taught the Beatitudes (vs. 11, "But the meek will inherit the land,"). By this quote, Jesus evoked the whole Psalm's message for His listeners. The radical life to which He was calling His disciples in the Sermon on the Mount, with all the difficulties it would create for their relationships, could be faced with an inner stillness, because of the inevitable exaltation of the meek and the destruction of the wicked.

Psalm 46 follows a similar logic. The Psalm paints a horrendous picture of the most extreme cataclysmic events imaginable: the "earth giv[ing] way" and "mountains fall[ing] into the heart of the sea" (vs. 2). It goes on: "Nations are in uproar, kingdoms fall" (vs. 6). And yet the Psalmist counsels the reader to "be still" (vs. 10). How is this possible? The Psalm begins and ends by showing God as deeply and powerfully *with* His people (vv. 1, 7, 11). The "river whose streams make glad the city of God," (vs. 4) is a picture of God Himself as Jerusalem's resource when under siege. The city has never had its own river, but God's presence within her (vs. 5) grants her all the benefits of a river. His presence guarantees that He will, "help her at break of day" (vs. 5). But most comforting of all, the Psalmist concludes with a reminder that God, "will be exalted among the nations, [God] will be exalted in the earth" (vs. 10). The reader can be still because, inevitably, God will be lifted up for all to see and will receive His due praise and honor.

This truth is how Jesus comforted Himself when He faced the cross. He set His mind on how His Father would be glorified by it. This allowed Him to proceed with the painful experience. "Now my soul is troubled, and what shall I say? 'Father, save, me from this hour?' No, it was for this very reason I came to this hour. Father, glorify your name!" (John 12:27-28). Jesus was motivated to continue toward the cross, and enabled to calmly face it, because He knew that by it God would be "exalted among the nations … exalted in the earth."

Likewise, you can learn to be still because God is with you and because He will inevitably be exalted. His agenda of enacting a just and righteous rule will finally reign triumphant and supreme over the face of the whole earth, no matter how much the nations collapse and the earth trembles. This remains true in our relationships, no matter how threatening they appear or how unsparingly they provoke our anxiety.

Like the Psalmist in Psalm 116:7-8, when threatened you can say to yourself: "Return to rest, O my soul, for the Lord has dealt bountifully with you. He has rescued your soul from death, your eyes from tears and your feet from stumbling." You can tell your soul to return to rest in the face of threat.

You don't even have to wait until an actual threat arises. You can practice this response of stillness and rest ahead of time. Imagine worst case scenarios and choose stillness while imagining them. For example, imagine your car failing you on the very day you can't afford to be without a car. Now play out the scenario in your head of the worst possible consequences that follow the car's failure. Exactly what are those consequences? How do they play out?

Doing this practice will reveal that the actual possibilities are not nearly as bad as the imaginary possibilities that spark the original panic. Then, when actual panic seizes you, you've already exercised that muscle a bit. Thus, when your car does fails, you've already rehearsed calmly walking through it.

This works in relationships as well as it works in your daily challenges. Imagine being still in the face of relational threats. A friendship threatens to engulf you by parasitically feeding on you. An interaction with a rude neighbor threatens to ruin your day. In all kinds of threats you can play out the worst case scenario in your head while calmly choosing stillness and telling your soul to return to its rest.

Practicing stillness in the face of relational threat will improve your level of differentiation. Your inward stillness is in direct proportion to your level of satisfaction with God. So the more satisfaction you can cultivate in God the less need you will have to fuse with others. The more still you can be when threatened, the more quickly you will bounce back with new strength afterwards. You will learn how to be a "non-anxious presence" in situations where everything seems to be falling apart.

Tip Four: Analyze Your Stuck Places

Every relationship gets stuck now and then. Husbands and wives, even those with very loving relationships, find themselves unable to progress relationally now and again. Parents and their children encounter seasons when they can't understand one another and they can't seem to get past their misunderstandings on their own. Best friends occasionally hit walls with each other in which they find it harder to relate to and empathize with each other. Many kinds of interactions can repeatedly provoke anxiety in us. And no relationship, no matter how loving, is without communication challenges.

To nurture your self-in-relation with the created, analyze these stuck places. By analyzing them you will discover exactly where and how God wants *you* to grow. When you feel as though you are drowning in your inability to move forward with another person, stop and analyze your stuck places.

This begins with noticing that you are in a stuck place. This isn't as easy as it sounds. Most people's first response to being stuck is to blame the other person. "We're struggling in our marriage because *she* can't understand my point of view." Blame shields us from looking within.

Now, it *is* possible that the fault lies completely with the other person. But this process isn't about discovering fault; it isn't even about fixing the relationship; it *is* about detecting where *you* need to become more differentiated and thus resilient.

Let's say that your current "stuck-ness" with your spouse really is "all her fault." We'll pretend it is for the moment. And even if it is, you need to come to a place of recognizing that in fact *you* are stuck. Whoever's fault it is, *you* are stuck and you can't get out on your own.

You know you're stuck when your relationship keeps you awake at night. You know you're stuck when your relationship causes you to go on tirades and rants about the other person, even if the tirade is all in your head. You know you're stuck when you rehearse an interaction several times after it occurred: "that was too awkward," "too uncomfortable," "too strained," "I just can't believe I let that out of my mouth – what must he think of me?" again and again and again. You know you're stuck when the words of the other person give you outsize emotions of any kind. In other words, maybe her words provoke strong sadness, or maybe strong worry, or maybe fierce anger, all out of proportion with the situation. You know you're stuck when you daydream about being with someone else. You know you're stuck when your relationship, or an interaction in that relationship, produces *any* anxiety in you, of any amount or degree of severity.

Once you recognize that you're stuck, you can begin to figure out what it is about *you* that has allowed you to get stuck. Now, we're still pretending that your spouse is completely to blame. Nevertheless, there is something inside of *you* that has permitted the other person to push your buttons this way.

For instance, let's say your spouse said something terribly insensitive in a recent interaction. She knew it was insensitive, and in fact she calculated her words to have exactly the effect of hurting your feelings. But what is it inside of *you* that finds the insensitive remark so terribly insensitive? We'll keep believing for a moment that your spouse was full of malice and intentional cruelty when she said what she said. We're not letting her off the hook for the moment. But again, what is it inside of *you* that was so wounded by the comment? Why did her words have such power over you? Would the exact same words have been as powerful coming from someone else?

Certainly there is a lot of history behind the remark. We don't doubt that for an instant. Almost certainly she should have known better than to say that to you. But why did you need her unconditional validation, understanding, empathy and high regard so much in the first place? Her comment violated you so deeply because you already believed she owed you that high regard. Why?

"Now wait a minute" you might object at this point. "Are you saying that my wife can go off and say whatever insensitive thing she wants, whenever she wants, without repercussions?" No, we're not saying that all. Remember, we believe you that it truly is all her fault. And we're not suggesting that she can get away with it.

"But are you implying that my feelings don't matter? You're saying that it's OK to blame the victim?" Again, no. Justice is a very serious matter, but for the moment your need for justice is getting in the way of discovering exactly where *you* need to differentiate.

You see, something inside of *you*, at some point in the relationship, gave your wife power over you. Something in you exchanged your *self*-respect for *wife*-respect. In other words, instead of being able to validate, comfort and soothe yourself in partnership with the Holy Spirit and with the truth of God, you unknowingly handed your wife the responsibility to validate, comfort and soothe your anxieties.

"But isn't that normal?" you object again. "Isn't it a sign of intimacy when two people can hurt each other so badly? Are you saying that husbands and wives shouldn't feel it deeply when they hurt each other? You're saying I should shake off the comment as if my spouse were a mere stranger?"

It is normal that intimacy includes the possibility of hurting one another. But in this book we're talking about our ability to be resilient when we get hurt. A differentiated person (and a differentiated relationship) can recover from mutually caused wounds. A non-differentiated person (and a non-differentiated relationship), cannot.

It doesn't really matter why and when and how you handed over to another the responsibility to validate and comfort yourself. If you have done this, welcome to humanity. It is common and normal—a near universal human experience. The point is that another person now controls your sense of self, and it is time to take it back.

If you can notice when you're stuck then you have hope to heal and differentiate. It is exactly at this stuck place that you need to repair the breach.

For instance, if the nasty comment violated your belief that you are a capable person ("You idiot! You just can't do anything right, can you?") then you need to bolster your view of your created self. In other words, it is time to focus on celebrating your capacities. If the comment violated your belief that you are a dutiful person ("I can't ever depend on you to be responsible, can I?!"), then thank God for all the ways He has enabled you to be responsible.

We're not suggesting that you reinforce delusions you have about yourself. If you need to grow in some capacity, or if you should improve the follow-through of your duties, then don't deny the truth of the criticisms with self-delusion. But if your beliefs about your capacity or your dutifulness are based on truth and not on self-delusion, then you will discover inner resources, by the power of the Holy Spirit, to re-strengthen your sense of self by celebrating yourself in the face of the threat. The more you can partner with the truth and with the Spirit who lives inside of you to bolster your sense of self, the less violating your spouse's attacks will feel.

This can feel like heavy weight lifting at first. It is much harder to remind yourself of the truth about yourself than to blame the problem on another. But gradually, with practice, as you call on God's Spirit to work in you, you'll get better and better at it. To be ready for these inevitable challenges to your sense of self, it is wise to rehearse regularly the truths about your created and re-created self, as discussed in previous chapters.

But we've still not tackled the hardest question in the process: *why* do you care? This is a serious question. *Why* has this cruel remark gotten the best of you? *Why* is it so important to you that your spouse sees you as capable or as responsible in this area? *Why* do you need to manage *her* belief about you with such particularity? *Why* do you need so desperately to project a certain image of yourself for her consumption?

Next, ask yourself "what if?" What if she really does believe that you are an irresponsible or incapable person? So what? What is the worst that can happen? How is it such a loss to you? Just asking this question has the power to show you that in fact, you never did need your spouse's approval in the first place.

Now comes the most critical moment. You arrive at this realization that your beloved spouse's regard for you cannot and should not control you. You've faced the awful truth that she does not hold you in the same high regard that you believe you deserve. This is now the moment to comfort yourself with the truths about who God is.

So, if your spouse does not care about you as you feel she ought, God does. In fact, God's care for you far surpasses any care you've ever imagined before. As you accept His care and love, you can release your need for your spouse's care and love.

This does not mean that your spouse gets off the hook. She still has something of which to repent. We're still blaming her for the whole problem. But what you've done is remove her control over your sense of self. You've handed it back to God who is truly able to love you unconditionally. In partnership with the Holy Spirit, you've told yourself the truth about you and about God's love for you. This has freed your feet from the shackles of depending on another's approval. You and God have freed yourself from the bondage of fusion.

We've still not solved the problem of your spouse's misbehavior. But you and God have opened the way for *you* to be resilient. If your spouse no longer has control over your sense of self, that leaves you free to heal and come back stronger.

A wonderful benefit to this process is that, because of your newfound freedom and resilience, you will be able to discern more clearly who is actually at fault. You'll be able to step back and observe the conflict rationally and objectively, as if you were a third party observer. Now you're free to find out in what ways you both have probably shared some blame in the situation.

Additionally, now you are calm and collected and able to handle the conflict constructively. Before you soothed yourself with the truth, stilling yourself in the face of threat, you were defensive and insecure and your negative emotions were ready to snap with a hair-trigger. But the process of comforting yourself with the truth has brought you into a calm state where you can relax and be rational.

Best of all, now you are in a place to love your spouse the way Jesus loves and the way He orders us to love. Freed from self-protectiveness you can reach out self-sacrificially and extend an empathic and caring olive branch to your spouse, because she can't hurt you any more. She's no longer a threat. Are there words of correction that you will need to say to her in order to repair the relationship? Is confrontation necessary to achieve real reconciliation? Now it is possible to say them effectively because you'll say them without the anger, self-defensiveness or accusative that would only increase the conflict. Now you can love incarnationally, like we explained in Chapter Five

Analyzing your stuck places requires you to get really good at self-awareness. To figure out where you're stuck and then to ask yourself these probing questions about your needs and your motives means that you've got to improve your ability to see into your own heart. It is difficult but the reward of resiliency and loving incarnationally makes the process of differentiation worth it.

Tip Five: Follow the Trail of Anxiety

One of the most helpful ways we can analyze our stuck places and practice stillness in threat is to follow the trail of anxiety to its source every time we notice that a relationship, or any situation for that matter, causes a spike in anxiety.

Anxiety is just part of the body's alarm system indicating that something isn't right. But as when a car alarm goes off in a crowded parking lot, anxiety can throw us into a tailspin and make us feel as if the something that's not right is bigger than it really is.

Have you ever noticed those several panicked moments in the parking lot when many people fumble around for their keys at the same time in an attempt to quiet the alarm? At first, no one knows exactly whose alarm it is, so everybody is on the hunt to stop it. Eventually, someone figures it out, the alarm is quieted and the rest of the people relax.

Anxiety can do the same to us. It can throw our entire inner life into disarray. And we're not always very good at uncovering the source of the alarm.

But there is a way for well-differentiated people to take a deep breath and calmly locate the real cause of the alarm instead of fumbling around in distress.

Surprisingly, the very alarm bells that cause such panic are the same trails that lead to the relational fusion at the source of it all. By following these trails of anxiety we can discover exactly what differentiation work we have yet to do and then do it.

Let's say you see "*that* person's" number come up on your phone. He is the last person you care to talk to right now. The mere thought of talking to that person produces anxiety. You feel the anxiety surge and you do whatever it takes to avoid dealing with him. But avoidance hasn't really calmed your anxiety because every time you think of him, even a little bit, you feel choked with more anxiety.

To grow in differentiation, see this as an opportunity rather than as a threat. It is an opportunity for growth and emotional maturity. It is an opportunity to become more like Jesus who models differentiated relationships.

When the anxiety arises, begin to ask yourself what makes you so anxious about talking to this person. Sometimes it is obvious (he yelled angrily at you in your most recent encounter). But most of the time it isn't obvious, and we're not even willing to admit that it is anxiety that we're feeling.

Still, it is important to take a deep breath and ask, "Where is this anxiety coming from?" Merely asking the question will calm down your nervous system and slow your racing brain and emotions.

Now, in this moment, invite God into the situation and pose the question to *Him*. Allow His Spirit to put His finger on the cause of the anxiety.

You could be anxious because talking to this person will produce a lot of work for you. You could be anxious because this person represents something distasteful or worrisome. You could be anxious because you've got to be the "bad guy" with this person and that tears away at your good guy self-image. You could be anxious because in your heart of hearts you know you have not done right by this person and you don't feel ready to face your own sin.

Whatever the cause of the anxiety, follow the trail of anxiety to its source. If you're honest with God and honest with yourself in following the trail, inevitably you will discover the real cause behind it.

How does this help us differentiate? First, once you are dealing with reality (anxiety would prefer we deal with fantasy and ghosts), you have something concrete to do about it instead of just squirm in apprehension. You can't win a boxing match against a shadow, but there is a possibility of winning if you box something real.

Second, you will discover the precise point where you must grow in differentiation. Have your over-identified with this person's favor or disfavor? Anxiety will show you the exact spot where you are fused. Does this person hold some sort of power over your sense of self? Anxiety will show you the exact spot where you've allowed him to have that power.

Even though anxiety generally produces a cloud around the places where we need to differentiate — a cloud that throws us into paralyzing confusion like all those car alarms going off at once — it will also unfailingly show us its source if we calmly follow its trail.

Third, you learn that this person isn't as big of a threat as you had feared. Once you've located the source of the anxiety trail, you can soothe yourself and say to yourself, "I'm actually not going to lose *everything* by interacting with this person." In other words, you gain insight into what this person holds over you and you see that God promises to preserve you through the threatened loss. Will he cause you to lose sleep? Peace of mind? Your self-congratulating image of yourself? Will his disfavor tarnish your sense of identity?

Whatever he may be able to do to you, you will find that God promises to see you through it. You realize that you can live without this person's favor and that you can rise above his disfavor. Even if your very life is at risk, God has promised you eternal life and that can't be taken away.

All this allows you to disentangle your sense of self, your identity, from the other person's control. This is differentiation.

Tip Six: Keep the Main Goal in Mind

The most important tip for nurturing your self-in-relation with the created is to keep the main relational goal always in mind: to love others as Christ loved us, incarnationally (John 13:34, 15:12).

Our earlier talk about boundaries may have led you to think our message is about avoiding intimacy. But the opposite is actually true. This chapter is all about relational intimacy. It is about growing up emotionally so you can obey Jesus' command: "love your neighbor as much as you love yourself" (Matt. 22:39). It's about gaining the maturity to imitate Jesus' love: "love one another *as I* have loved you" (John 13:34, 15:12).

This means being free from the internal barriers that prevent us from loving another person in the way God desires. It means being free from the control of fears, anxieties, repulsions and feelings of threat that rise up when we consider being in close relationship with another person. It also means being free to say "no" to inappropriate attraction that are aroused when we are in a relationship with another.

"But won't I achieve relational intimacy if I can just stay vigilant against my own sins? Aren't my sins the main obstacle to human intimacy?" you may ask. This is certainly true and is affirmed throughout the Bible. Vigilance against your sins is a necessary part of growing your capacity to love. In fact, it is foundational and if you do not pay attention to the damage your sinful nature can cause you will never come close to relational intimacy. Christianity has always prescribed that you consciously purge yourself of sin with the help of God's Spirit and guided by His truth in Scripture, especially in regard to the effect of sin on your relationships. Your sin is always the first thing to identify when you attempt to move past the obstacles that prevent your intimacy with others.

But we're talking about freedom from the things that "so easily entangle" (Hebrews 12:1-2). These are the things, in addition to sin but that work in tandem with sin, that threaten to prevent our obedience to love as Jesus commands. This involves a lot more than just ridding yourself of known sins.

We're talking first of all about increasing your self-awareness. Self-awareness is necessary so that you can see the threat of fusion from far off and so you can strategize how to successfully dodge it. Seeing the threat from afar is necessary so that you realize ahead of time how you will likely react to relational threats of all kinds, both the scary ones and the enticing ones.

This step is necessary so that you know what to do with all the emotions and thoughts that rise up inside of you when you face these threats. Imagine all the sin that is prevented when we can side step the emotions that "so easily entangle" and that tend to drag us into sin.

After self-awareness, you need to grow in your ability to soothe and comfort yourself in the face of relational threats. You need to be able to do this when a relationship appears frightening or you will unthinkingly revert to inappropriate "fight or flight" responses. Repeating short, biblical phrases like, "God is my refuge and my strength, an ever present help in trouble (Ps. 46:1)" or "The Lord is my light and my salvation—whom shall I fear (Ps. 27:1)" or "Return to rest, O my souls" (Ps. 116:7) can be marvelously helpful in comforting yourself when another person appears as though he can steal something precious from your very identity.

You also need to be able to comfort yourself in the face of threats that appear more enticing. For example, let's say you feel drawn into an inappropriate relationship. You need to learn how to respond with more than simply cutting it off or avoiding it or putting up boundaries. That's one important step but it's not enough to help you stay free of the enticement. You are drawn into it because a part of you feels as if you were missing something important to your happiness or because you feel as if God were doing a poor job of caring for your needs. So you've got to learn how to fight back by comforting yourself with God's truth.

A part of you will try to convince yourself that, "life would be so much better if I were in a relationship with her. I would feel so much more satisfied and supported and alive." You counteract this by comforting yourself: "life is actually better without this relationship. I've got all the resources I need to feel satisfied, supported and alive. God has provided for all my emotional needs." If you do not know how to comfort yourself like this in the face of relational threats you will not have the capacity for authentic, intimate relationships. The truths in Psalm 16 are a great place to begin.

The capacity to love ultimately involves the emotional faculty to not overly-depend on the approval of or disapproval of others. It requires you to free yourself from the default tendency to fuse with others. Fusion threatens to make all relationships, even apparently close ones, exploitative. So you've got to learn to be free from it if you hope to acquire the capacity to love as Jesus did.

If you ignore your tendency to fuse and only focus on uprooting your sins you'll always be disappointed with your inability to be intimate. You may do an excellent job of keeping your heart pure of sin before God. But if you don't grow in freedom from the tendency to fuse you will keep struggling with the same problem over and over again.

Above all, this capacity involves learning how, like Jesus, to faithfully hold on to your true self — your created and re-created self — while still entering the reality of another, for their benefit. This is incarnation. Only a truly differentiated relationship, in which both parties are growing in differentiation, has the possibility for this kind of incarnational intimacy. The more differentiated your relationships with others are, the more resilient you will be.

The more you gain this inner capacity to have differentiated relationships with others, the more you will treasure humans for their own sake, in imitation of Jesus' example and in response to His command to love as He loved. You will have greater capacity to be "incarnational," to hold on to both your created and re-created self and to enter into the reality of other people in an empathetic and self-sacrificing way.

Differentiation will give greater capacity to be in loving relationships with God's community, the Church, despite all her failings, shortcomings, and immaturity. You will be able to throw in your lot with God's people as He requires of you, as daunting as that seems. What's more, you will be able to lead God's people with love as He has called you to lead them because their pettiness or even viciousness will no longer threaten the core *you*.

When emotionally immature people react negatively to your leadership you will have the capacity to remain calm and to be at peace. When you encounter hard-to-navigate ethnically and culturally diverse relationships you'll be able to remain open hearted and open-minded. When those you lead run into problems because of your leadership mistakes, instead of throwing up all kinds of defenses and obfuscations to distract others from whose fault it is, you will have the inner calm to look soberly at your own contributions to the problems. Overall, you will be more resilient so that you can continue to love others as Christ has loved you. Always keep this main goal in mind as you seek to increase your level of differentiation.

Summary

In this chapter we have given you several tips for how best to nurture your self-in-relation with the Creator and the created. We've recommended that you make peace with God's mysteriousness, delight in His delightfulness, embrace His sovereignty, and practice submission and surrender to God. We've also counseled you to treasure others for their own sake, to hold on to yourself, to practice stillness

in the face of threat, to analyze your stuck
places, to follow the trail of anxiety to its source
and to keep the main goal in mind, which is to
love incarnationally as Christ loved.

Chapter Ten:
Alfonso, Petr and Jennifer

It was completely dark by the time Alfonso and Jennifer pulled off I-465 and onto Crawfordsville Road. Neither of them had spent much time on this side of town except when the city was gearing up for the Indy 500, so the neighborhood was almost unrecognizable now without all the Race promotions.

"I remember Petr's stories of how, as a kid, he'd con Race-goers out of money just for information about parking," Al said in an attempt to find something light to discuss. They'd both been nearly mute while driving from the coffee shop to here. Both were experiencing a growing sense of dread as they drew closer to the old, run down apartment building where Svetlana had raised Petr.

It took a while to find it. The darkness blurred the distinctions between the various apartment buildings, and at first Jennifer wasn't 100% certain which block it was on. She found her memory was scattered about the details but she knew it had to be one among only a few different options.

"Wow," said Alfonso, as they cruised slowly up and down along several blocks, "This neighborhood is pretty dumpy without all the Race fanfare."

"I thought you'd been here several times to visit Svetlana, back before she moved in with us?" Jen interjected. She was starting to panic a bit about locating the right building.

"Just once, right after we graduated from seminary. We drove here together straight from seminary so I could help Petr move the rest of his stuff into his new apartment. But to be honest, I have no memory of seeing the surrounding neighborhood. And I guess, besides that, I've never been here when it wasn't Race Day."

"Well, it's gotten a lot better, even though you might not be able to tell from this street. Overall, I think Indianapolis has done pretty well for itself, in spite of the Great Recession and the big Coronavirus Pandemic."

"Ugh, the 'Great Recession!' The 'Pandemic!' I tell you, Jen, this last decade has really been awful to the people in my church. So many out of work, so many without enough work."

"Sorry to hear that, Al," Jen responded, trying to sound empathetic, even though her mind was obviously on other things. But she hoped that by thinking of someone else's problems for a moment, she might alleviate some of her own anxiety.

"I suppose all that has impacted what the church can pay you?" Petr's salary had been frozen during the Great Recession and then later in the Pandemic, but otherwise they'd felt little direct impact. Their congregation of mostly upper middle class Caucasian attenders had not felt the severity of these events to the same degree of more diverse congregations like Alfonso's.

"Yep," Alfonso began. "I had to take a big pay cuts to reflect the tithing abilities of our church members. We even had to start talking about me going to part time. But by God's grace…"

"There it is!" Jen yelled.

"Are you sure, Jen? It's really hard for me to tell in the dark like this."

"Yes…." Jen took a deep breath, "at least, I'm 90% confident."

"Well, that's better than nothing. Let's go." They pulled over and parked the car. They were one of only a few cars on the dimly lit block.

"That building looks all boarded up everywhere. And there's a lock on the fence around it. I wonder how we'll get in?" Al said this more to himself than to Jennifer since he knew he had to be the one to think through their next move. He could tell she was too anxious at the moment to do anything more than put one foot in front of the other.

After walking all the way around the building's exterior, they found a section in the back where the chain link didn't go as high as other parts of the fence. Alfonso turned to Jen with a grim look on his face and said, "Jen, I think this is the only way in." She nodded with the same grim look on her face.

Suddenly, a scream from behind them sent them twirling around, their hearts in their throats.

Jennifer screamed and grabbed her mouth with both hands.

Alfonso clenched his fists and walked into the gloom to see what was going on. He turned back to Jen, "It's OK Jen. It's just a raccoon facing off with a stray cat." Angry from being shocked so badly, Alfonso ran at the animals to chase them away. "Oh, man, that almost gave me heart attack. Are you OK?"

Jen nodded grimly again. She was silent for several seconds until her breathing began to return to normal. "Al, I'm really scared. What if we're ... what if we're too late? What if he's already done it? What if ..."

Alfonso grabbed her hand and began praying, "Lord, we need your help. If there is any chance that Petr's still alive, please, please, please direct us ..." After a few minutes he looked up and said, "Jen, I'm pretty sure, based on all the other clues, Petr's going to wait until his birthday, and I'm still pretty sure he's going to try it at church. I think there's a really good chance he's done nothing to himself yet." He was silent for a long time, and finally said. "I really hope I'm right. Let's go."

Jen nodded silently and followed Alfonso over the fence. It proved to be harder than either of them had anticipated. Once Alfonso's jeans caught on a broken piece of fencing. Then, while Alfonso was helping Jen make it down the last few feet, she suddenly froze.

"Al!" she called out in a harsh whisper. "I see somebody coming!"

About 100 yards away, by a set of rusted-out and overflowing dumpsters, they both saw a shadowy, human figure. Both found they couldn't move as they gazed intently into the darkness.

The figure stayed in one place for a long time, just out of reach of the nearby streetlight. Alfonso was just starting to wonder if he should call out Petr's name, but then the figure moved closer to the light.

The person's short, wide frame made it immediately clear that it wasn't Petr. He shuffled slowly as though he were very elderly or slightly disabled. He glanced briefly in the direction of Jennifer and Alfonso but either didn't notice them or didn't care. Judging from the old bag of fast food he was clutching, Alfonso guessed he'd just fished a meal out of the dumpster.

After Jennifer started breathing again, she jumped down the last bit of fence and then grabbed Alfonso's arm, "I don't think I can take another shock like that," she said quietly.

The two walked around to the front of the building, but discovered that the entire wood staircase leading up to Petr's childhood second story apartment had rotted away almost completely. There was no way up.

"Now what are we going to do?" Jen blurted out, more loudly than she'd intended.

"There has to be a fire escape in the back, right?" Al stated.

Walking around the back, they discovered an old metal fire escape that did not appear to be in much better condition than the front stairs. Alfonso was the first to hoist himself slowly up to the bottom rung, along with a mumbled comment about the 40s not being kind to his body. After crawling up to the first tiny landing, he turned around and reached down his arm to help Jennifer up.

Clawing up the rusty fire escape toward the second story was even harder than getting over the fence. But finally, they were facing the boarded up back window of the apartment.

"And we're sure this is the one?" Al asked one more time.

"Yes, yes, I'm certain now" Jen responded. "His and Svetlana's apartment was one in from the corner. I'm sure this is it."

Alfonso groped around the boarded up window with his fingers. It was so dark now that even with Jen's flashlight from her phone he couldn't rely on his eyes to assess the condition of the boards with accuracy. He felt his way carefully around the whole thing while giving the board little tugs and pushes. After a moment he found that the bottom half suddenly pealed easily away.

Turning to Jennifer he whispered "I'm pretty sure someone pried this off recently. The whole thing is no longer nailed to the frame. It was just resting here."

Jennifer nodded, swallowed down tears, and whispered hoarsely, "let's do it."

They pulled off the rest of the board, aimed their phone flashlights into the gloom of the open window, and started to crawl in.

"Petr?" Jen called out into the darkness.

Epilogue

Did they reach Petr in time?

We have deliberately left the ending of their story to your imagination. What do you think will happen to Petr? Was Petr beyond hope? Was his level of biblical differentiation so low that he was unable to be resilient in this current trial? Petr had neglected to nurture his created self, his re-created self, and his self-in-relation with God and others. Was he beyond hope?

Or had Alfonso's letters and Jennifer's rebukes gotten through to him? Would they be able to talk with him if they found him alive? Would they be able to persuade him to give up this attempt at suicide?

Whatever happens to Petr, this book is an invitation for you to pay attention to the work in front of *you*. How does all this apply to you? What about *your* own level of differentiation? Would you bounce back from similar trials? Would you persevere and become better than before? Or would you inwardly collapse like Petr did?

In the first chapter, we challenged you with the idea that "resilience" is just another word for the old fashioned biblical idea of perseverance. The Bible is unambiguous on the matter: every believer must learn how to persevere. Jesus (Matt. 24:13), Paul (Rom. 5:4, 1 Cor. 13:7, 2 Thess. 1:4), Peter (2 Pet. 1:6), the author of Hebrews (Heb. 10:36) and James (James 1:4) overwhelmingly agree that all Christians must become good at persevering. Paul gave Christian leaders an especially strong exhortation to persevere (1 Tim. 4:16). However much longer we must await Jesus' return, and whatever new trials and persecutions we must face as Christians, we must learn how to persevere. Will you? Will you influence those you lead to persevere?

If, in partnership with your Creator, you will nurture the three legs of biblical differentiation—your created self, your re-created self, and your self-in-relation with the Creator and the created—then you will by God's grace set yourself up to be a resilient leader when trials and difficulties come. You will better train yourself and your followers to persevere.

We also challenged you with the idea that God wants you to love as He loves (John 13:34, 15:12, Eph. 5:1-2). He wants us to love incarnationally, in imitation of His love for us. But our lack of differentiation throws up all kinds of obstacles to loving that way so that, no matter vigilant we've been to eliminate obvious sin from our lives, we fail to lovingly comfort and confront like Jesus did. How will you love incarnationally when your inner life resists doing so?

If, in partnership with your Creator, you nurture biblical differentiation, then you have more hope to imitate Jesus' incarnational love for other people. What's more, you will better lead others to imitate Jesus' Incarnation as well.

Of course, biblical differentiation in these three areas is a continual process, one from which you never fully graduate. Once you make progress in the differentiation of one relationship, another one awaits in the wings. You'll never be done with this journey until Christ returns, so stay on guard. Remember how Joshua was deceived by the Gibeonites (Josh. 9), despite all his maturity and experience.

But even though there are obstacles and difficulties on the way toward improving your level of differentiation, ultimately this is a rewarding journey. It is a journey that glorifies God above all. It glorifies Him because your incarnational living will point back to Jesus' Incarnation. And it will glorify God because, as you grow, you will increasingly see that it was His mercy and goodness that has led you all the way through this wilderness and into the Promised Land.

Made in the USA
Monee, IL
01 July 2020